# THE NOBEL PRIZE
## ANNUAL
## 1990

# THE NOBEL PRIZE
# ANNUAL
# 1990

ISBN 0-8161-7376-1

©1991 International Merchandising Corporation
22 East 71st Street
New York, New York 10021

The Nobel Prize Annual 1990 was developed by IMG
Publishing with the assistance of The Nobel Foundation.
The copyright to the original texts of the presentation
speeches and lectures, from which extracts are quoted,
belongs to the Foundation.

Photography by Lars Aström

Original Cover and Interior Design by
Michaelis/Carpelis Design Assoc. Inc.
Project Editor:  Campbell Geeslin

Printed in the United States of America

# CONTENTS

*A bust of Alfred Nobel stands outside his Björkborn Manor House, today a museum, in Karlskoga, Sweden.*

E ach year, more than 2,000 significant awards are given internationally, but none carries the prestige or attracts the worldwide attention of the gold medal bearing the profile of Alfred Nobel. During the last nine decades, the Nobel Prize has been awarded to the citizens of 38 countries and has had broad influence in each of the areas it honors. It has brought to the forefront new ideas in science and medicine—and reminded governments and corporations of the importance of their financial aid to keep these discoveries coming. The Peace Prize, despite its sometimes controversial choices, invariably has called attention to the major problems of the world. And, over the years, the prize for literature has significantly widened the influence of writing from such countries as Spain, Germany, Italy, Belgium, Norway, Great Britain, Ireland, and the United States.

This volume introduces us to the achievements of the fascinating group of 1990 laureates: a trio of physicists who found a new rung on the ladder of creation; a chemist whose medicines improve the health of all; two doctors who pioneered human transplants; a humble poet from Mexico whose work touches people everywhere; three economists who made sense of financial markets; and a Soviet leader who decided that, after 40 years of domination, it was time to let Eastern Europe taste freedom.

By presenting these portraits of those who have received the Nobel Prize in 1990, Ernst & Young hopes to inspire others who, through the brilliance of their ideas in medicine and literature, economics and humanitarianism, will benefit all of mankind.

*Ernst & Young*

*The 1990 Nobel laureates (front row) stand as the prize presentation ceremony begins.*

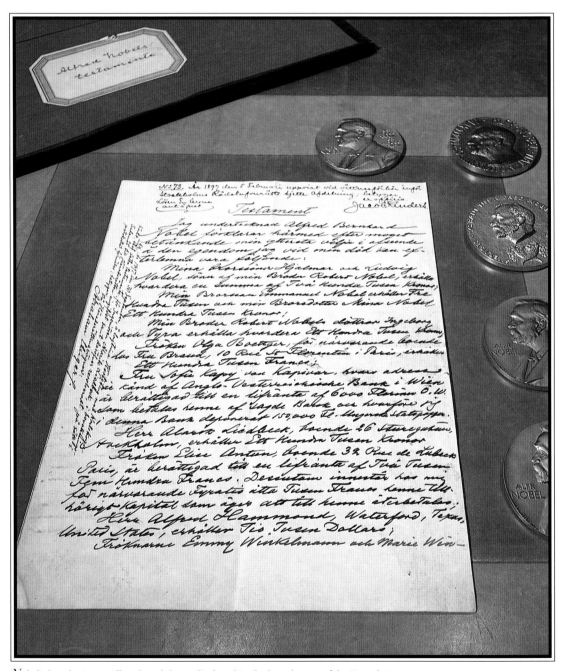

*Nobel's handwritten will and medals are displayed in the board room of the Foundation.*

# GORBACHEV & TEN 'AMERICANS'

**STIG RAMEL**
*President of the Nobel Foundation*

The Peace Prize was undoubtedly the most talked-about Nobel award of 1990. Speculations in the news media were already abundant at the beginning of the year, and most of the items focused on President Mikhail Gorbachev, as it was known that he had received an unusually high number of nominations. The Nobel institutions never make nominations public: According to the Nobel statutes, these nominations should be kept secret for fifty years. But those who make nominations for the Peace Prize—among those eligible to do so, members of national legislatures all over the world dominate—nearly always make their nominations public. It seems to be a part of the game.

When the prize to President Gorbachev was officially announced on October 15, it caused a sensation, even though it had been expected. The man who had opened the gates for peaceful change in Eastern Europe could not, however, go to Oslo

for the ceremonies on December 10, for the political situation in Moscow made his attendance impossible. It is ironic that the only other Nobel peace laureates from Eastern Europe, Andrei Sakharov (1975) and Lech Walesa (1983), could not go to Oslo either. In their cases, too, the political situation in Moscow had cast its shadow across the awards ceremony.

In Stockholm, December 10, the anniversary of Alfred Nobel's death, was celebrated in the traditional way. The ten laureates in physics, chemistry, physiology or medicine, literature, and economics were all on the stage at the Stockholm Concert Hall. They all came from the New World: eight from the United States, one from Canada, and one from Mexico. Why so many Americans? The reason is that all of the 1990 prizes in the sciences were given for breakthroughs made in the 1950s or 1960s, when the American dominance of world science was at its height.

The Nobel Prize in physics was given to

Professors Jerome I. Friedman, Henry W. Kendall, and Richard E. Taylor "for their pioneering investigations concerning deep inelastic scattering of electrons on protons and bound neutrons, which have been of essential importance for the development of the quark model in particle physics." The three laureates had opened doors to the inner structure of protons and neutrons, using the three-mile-long accelerator at Stanford Linear Accelerator Center (SLAC) in California. The European accelerator at CERN (the European Organization for Nuclear Research) had served a similar function for Nobel Prize winners in the 1980s.

Even if particle physics will in the long run have an impact on everyone's daily life, the 1990 Nobel Prizes in chemistry and physiology or medicine are particularly close to Alfred Nobel's wish—expressed in his will—that the prizes should be given to "those who shall have conferred the greatest benefit to mankind."

Professor Elias J. Corey, cited "for his development of the theory and methodology of organic synthesis," created the basis for synthetic production of some hundreds of important natural products, not only of scientific but also of great practical importance. The physiology or medicine prize to Professors Joseph E. Murray and E. Donnall Thomas for their discoveries of "organ and cell transplantation in the treatment of human disease" also meets Nobel's standard. Their discoveries have saved the lives of thousands all over the world.

One of Professor Thomas's patients, the great Spanish opera singer José Carreras, was prevented from going to Stockholm to honor the man who saved his life only because of a long-standing engagement with the Vienna State Opera. Great singers belong to the rare category of people who cannot change their schedules in order to attend a Nobel awards ceremony.

The work of the three recipients of the Bank of Sweden's Prize in Economic Sciences in Memory of Alfred Nobel, Professors Harry M. Markowitz, Merton H. Miller, and William F. Sharpe, also has had an impact on people's day-to-day lives, especially investors. They were cited "for their pioneering work in the theory of financial economics." I am proud to say that the Nobel Foundation has for many years followed the investment policies recommended by the laureates, stressing the importance of diversifying investments and "not putting all our eggs in one basket." We had done so even before learning of the laureates' theories. Thanks to the foresight of the Foundation, they now share a prize of four million Swedish kronor (about $700,000)—the highest prize sum ever, but at the same time considerably smaller than the prize sum will be in 1991.

As always, the Nobel Prize in literature is especially close to most people's hearts and minds. Long before receiving the Nobel Prize, Dr. Octavio Paz had achieved great stature far beyond the literary world of the Spanish-speaking nations. His prize was awarded "for impassioned writing with wide horizons, characterized by sensuous intelligence and humanistic integrity." His personality, marked by humanity and compassion, endeared him to all who made his acquaintance during the Nobel celebrations. Like his colleagues, Octavio Paz met not only the King and Queen, the Prime Minister, and other leading members of Swedish society but also hundreds of students when he visited universities and hundreds of readers when he signed his books at a bookstore.

This is the true essence of the Nobel Week in Stockholm—to enable people to encounter the laureates not only through books, newspapers, and television but also face-to-face and mind-to-mind. ■

*Swedish film star Max Von Sydow congratulated literature laureate Octavio Paz.*

# THE NOBEL PRIZE
## ANNUAL
## 1990

# NOBEL HOUSE

## PHOTOGRAPHS BY LARS ASTROM

A friend once described Alfred Nobel as "a thinker, a poet, a man
bitter and good, unhappy and
gay—given to superb flights of mind and
to malicious suspicions, passionately in
love with the far horizons of human thought
and profoundly distrustful of the pettiness
of human folly, understanding everything
and hoping for nothing."

It is easy to imagine such a man at
Björkborn Manor House, which he bought
in 1893. It lies just outside the village of
Karlskoga, 155 miles from Stockholm, three
hours by train.

Both the house and Nobel's nearby
laboratory are museums, open to the public
during June, July, and August and at other
times by special arrangement. Most of the
furnishings are original, selected and pur-
chased by Nobel's nephew Hjalmar Nobel.

Nobel imported three Russian stallions
to draw the carriage in which he rode
about Karlskoga. The elegant vehicle had
rubber-covered wheels, a telephone used
to speak to the driver, and an electric
accumulator that lit the coach and the
horses' harness.

*"Europe's richest vagabond"—an epithet he earned
by living in so many countries—stayed at
Björkborn Manor House when he visited his
factory in Sweden. He had a laboratory
nearby, which is also a museum.*

Nobel allowed himself to be photographed only with great reluctance. He was even less enthusiastic about having his portrait painted, but did allow one to be done and sat for it in his laboratory. At the right is the dining room. When Sweden's King Oscar II was a houseguest, he made a speech praising Alfred Nobel and his family, but later the king was unhappy about Nobel's will, thinking the prizes should have been for Swedes only.

Nobel had a desk in his bedroom at Björkborn Manor. His controversial will, which set up the prizes, was filed for probate in a small local court nearby. Below. The bedstead of rich woods was hand carved. Opposite: Nobel's glasses lie on an open copy of the best-selling novel, Down with Arms, by the 1905 Peace Prize laureate Bertha von Suttner. The 1889 book helped initiate a major peace movement in Europe. This copy, a gift from the author, reveals many passages underlined by Nobel. ∎

*George Bernard Shaw was awarded a Nobel Prize in 1925 "for his work which is marked by both idealism and humanity. . . ."*

# CHAPTER 1

# NINE DECADES OF PRIZE-WINNING DRAMA

**by William A. Henry III**

*Four Nobelists are unquestioned luminaries of the theater: George Bernard Shaw, Luigi Pirandello, Eugene O'Neill, and Samuel Beckett. Even today one cannot imagine a stage season in any cultural capital without a work by at least one—and perhaps all—of them. This essay is by the Pulitzer Prize-winning theater critic for* Time *magazine.*

What do Henrik Ibsen, August Strindberg, Anton Chekhov, Bertolt Brecht, Federico García Lorca, Maxim Gorky, Jean Genet, Tennessee Williams, Arthur Miller, and Athol Fugard have in common? Apart from being a virtual who's who of twentieth-century giants of the theater admired in their own right, deeply influential on their successors, and still produced around the world, they share the unhappy distinction of not having won the Nobel Prize in literature.

They are, of course, in distinguished company (think of Tolstoy and Mark Twain), and there are ameliorative explanations. Some died early in the century, when the award was new and the Swedish Academy faced a plethora of choices. Some died abruptly and young, before they could be honored at the customary time, in the autumnal, summing-up season of life. Some behaved badly in their personal lives and may thus have been judged unsuitable, whatever their gifts. Some are still alive and may yet win. And, of course, in this century the drama has been far outpaced by the novel as the primary means of literary expression, not least because the new (and not Nobel-eligible) dramatic forms of film and television have enticed away some superior talents who in prior generations would have graced the stage; hence, fiction writers increasingly dominate the prizes. A conspicuous measure of the decline of the playwright is that four of the first thirteen Nobel winners in literature were known in substantial measure as stage writers, as against only one among the past twenty-two. Yet after all these considerations have been acknowledged, it is still striking how vast a range of the foremost dramatists of the Nobel Prize era have been overlooked by the prize's grantors. The omitted artists very nearly overshadow the recipients.

Ibsen and Strindberg were reportedly deemed lacking in moral uplift, although Ibsen now stands as the very symbol of the socially committed, humanistic artist, and Strindberg epitomizes liberating candor about the torments of married life. Chekhov is the model of the artist concerned with the dignity of the individual and Brecht, the beau ideal of the artist as communitarian crusader. In the late twentieth century, no consciences have been more imaginatively inflamed than those of Miller and Fugard. Gorky, the committed Communist, and Lorca, Williams, and Genet, the self-perceived homosexual rebels, made political points with their lives and poetic ones

in their works.

Nine writers actually have been honored with the Nobel Prize in literature in large part for their dramatic works. (Many other winners who are known primarily as novelists, essayists, or poets, including T. S. Eliot, Jean-Paul Sartre, William Butler Yeats, and Isaac Bashevis Singer, also provided works for the stage at some point in their long careers.) Four of the drama Nobelists are unquestioned luminaries: George Bernard Shaw, Luigi Pirandello, Eugene O'Neill, and Samuel Beckett. Even today one cannot imagine a stage season in any cultural capital without work by at least one and perhaps all of them. The other five, however — Björnstjerne Björnson of Norway, José Echegaray of Spain, Maurice Maeterlinck of Belgium, Gerhart Hauptmann of Germany, and Wole Soyinka of Nigeria — are not so widely known outside (and, in Hauptmann's case, even inside) their homelands. To be sure, celebrity does not equate with merit, as the Nobel grantors have repeatedly emphasized. And reputations that have faded occasionally recoup: It happened to Herman Melville, so it might happen to Maeterlinck. But at present, even the most diligent theater critic in New York City, London, or Paris might well need a lifetime to manage to see works by even two or three of this unsung quintet.

A major reason for their relative invisibility is that four of them thrived

*Norway's Björnstjerne Björnson was cited in 1903 "as a tribute to his noble, magnificent and versatile poetry."*

duced and a further decade away from mounting his masterwork, known in English as *Six Characters in Search of an Author*. O'Neill was a boy of twelve in 1900, and Beckett would not be born for another six years. They were all men of their century, preoccupied with stripping away illusion — political, psychological, or metaphysical — to expose the raw nerves of the human condition. In style and subject this quartet may not have had much in common. Shaw, at one extreme, was the quintessential man of affairs, as much partisan politician and speechmaker as writer. Beckett, at the other pole, was profoundly withdrawn, so reclusive that he tried to resist the Nobel and agreed to accept it only in absentia. Shaw's plays spurt fountains of debate masquerading as dialogue; Beckett's verge on the mute. But they share with the family-obsessed O'Neill and the gossip-scarred Pirandello a characteristic indignation. These four helped define what became the essentials of Western drama — bafflement and anger.

Every writer, however much he innovates, owes an immeasurable debt to those who went before. As more than one aphorist has remarked, a novice writer is nothing other than a reader moved by enthusiasm to the act of imitation. Some writers consciously rebel from this duty to heritage; others live in thrall to it. All must cope with it, because the legacy of the distant and recent past affects the most im-

mostly in the nineteenth century or the first few years of the twentieth, as much last gasps of romanticism as harbingers of modernism. The fifth shaped his career primarily in the context of Africa, placing himself, even during exile, at a remove from the mainstream of Western European traditions and customs.

Shaw, by contrast, had half a century left to live and fulminate when 1900 arrived. Pirandello was a decade away from seeing his first play pro-

portant variable in literature, the expectations of audiences. Thus, every playwright of the twentieth century, even those who have never read any of his works, is an heir of the first playwright to win the Nobel Prize, Björnstjerne Björnson, who was also known as a poet, journalist, and novelist when he won in 1903. Anger and bafflement are not precisely the words that come to mind when reading Björnson, who evolved from a bard of rural life into an optimistic advocate of urban liberal reform in ways that anticipated and seemingly inspired his contemporary, Ibsen. If one were to name a single playwright of the nineteenth century who most influenced the twentieth, Ibsen would be rivaled only by Chekhov and perhaps the German expressionist Georg Büchner. Yet in his compassion and commitment to making a better society, Björnson paved the way for Ibsen and thus foretokened the drama of the century to come.

Born in 1832 in the bleak uplands in the Kvikne district but sent in his youth to live in the lush Romsdal valley, he seemed all his life to believe something better was just around the corner. As the *Oxford Companion to the Theatre* says of him, "His biographers have remarked upon the joy and delight with which Björnson, as a child, looked at the new and unexpected beauty of the world to which he found himself transferred, and something from the mood of that moment seems

to have remained with him throughout his life." Ardently religious, he had a believer's faith in the perfectibility of man and society; he once effused, "Where good men walk, there are God's ways." Perhaps it was this optimistic, affirmative side that early Nobel grantors preferred to Ibsen's dour pessimism. It seemingly endeared him to fellow Norwegians, who have placed a statue of him outside the National Theater in Oslo, an honor otherwise accorded only to Ibsen. (Despite a natural rivalry, the two were friends. Indeed, after Björnson traveled in southern Europe to intellectual advantage, he discreetly helped finance Ibsen on a similar voyage.)

Björnson's dramatic career, which included practical experience running theaters in Bergen and Christiania (now Oslo), produced a sequence of four genres altogether typical of later nineteenth-century artists. His earliest efforts were celebrations of rural life, and it is these pieces, now purely nostalgic, that remain best known in Norway today, albeit more in fiction than in drama. One such novella, *The Happy Boy*, opens with the sentence, "Eivind was his name, and he cried when he was born." According to Oslo theater professionals, that line is as familiar to their countrymen as "To be or not to be..." is to the English-speaking world. Next in Björnson's development came patriotic and nationalistic works, of particular importance to a country that had spent centuries

*José Echegaray of Spain shared the 1904 prize because he had "revived the great traditions of the Spanish drama."*

under Danish or Swedish domination and had not yet gained its independence. Then came explorations of society's moral decay that presaged Ibsen's harsher accusations, and last came inward-looking spiritual journeys. Of his socially conscious works, the most highly regarded today are the plays known in English as *A Bankruptcy* and *The Editor,* both dating from 1875. The former deals with business

ethics, the latter with the predatory press, both fertile topics for many later dramatists, including Shaw and Pirandello. Like them, Björnson also wrote about the relationship between present love and past scandal, debating whether marriage ought to take into account such societal values as reputation. Of his later spiritual studies, the chief was *Beyond Human Power.* Its first part, produced in 1883, portrays a pastor who can heal problems in his church but not at home; the sequel, produced in 1895, concerns struggles between capital and labor, and the links to the first play are elusive.

The year after Björnson won the Nobel Prize in literature, the award went to another septuagenarian, José Echegaray of Spain (who shared it with Frédéric Mistral of France). His selection reflects the zeal of the romantic nineteenth century for melodramas on grand themes of honor and duty. To less sentimental and more cynical modern audiences, most of Echegaray's sixty or so plays are scholarly curiosities, noteworthy for the way in which they retain virtually up to the present most of the form and rhetoric of Spain's swashbuckling seventeenth-century Golden Age drama. About half are even written in verse. In terms of English-language theater, it is as though Shaw had been a near contemporary of Marlowe. Yet Shaw certainly felt admiration, if not kinship, toward Echegaray. When one of

Echegaray's plays was performed under the title *Folly or Saintliness* in 1895, Shaw hailed the tale about a character of an integrity so unyielding that he is considered insane, describing its author as "of the school of Schiller, Victor Hugo and Verdi—picturesque, tragic to the death, showing us the beautiful and the heroic struggling either with blind destiny or with an implacable idealism which makes vengeance and jealousy national points of honor." When Echegaray retold the heritage-of-dissoluteness story of one of Shaw's favorite Ibsen plays, *Ghosts,* in a piece known in English as *The Son of Don Juan,* the English writer applauded alterations in dramatis personae and plot that, he said, made the Spanish version "perfectly original" rather than a mere pastiche of the Norwegian. The disappearance of the indignant mother and horrified pastor and the placing at center stage of a corrupt patriarch, Shaw wrote, "will make it plain to anyone who had really comprehended *Ghosts* that the story has been taken on to new ground nationally, and back to old ground morally."

An engineer, mathematician, and sometime government minister, Echegaray apparently entered playwriting in adolescence to compete with a younger brother, Miguel, who was first produced as a child prodigy and went on to become a comedist of some note. The elder Echegaray, born in 1832, was undeniably facile but, in the judgment of many critics, sloppy and shallow. His own countrymen were far from unanimously pleased when he was chosen for the Nobel Prize. Yet all found him a master of theatrical effect and a dedicated reformer. Stage historian George Freedley wrote, "Despite all his extravagance and claptrap, his shoddiness and frequent triviality, Echegaray was a moralist and employed the drama to prove his points." Even Freedley unstintingly admired what is generally accepted as Echegaray's masterwork, translated literally as *The Great Galeoto* but also known in English as *Calumny.* Said Freedley, "The crusader in Ibsen naturally appealed to him, so it is no mere coincidence that his best play comes closest to the social dramas of the great Norwegian. This is a thesis play with a real social problem, that of the evil effects that befall a family when thoughtless or malicious gossip is spread." In the end, a woman unjustly accused of being a man's mistress decides that she might as well live up, or down, to her reputation.

Other critics have seen behind Echegaray's traditionalism some hints of modernity. They have likened him specifically to Pirandello for their shared fondness for questioning the nature of reality, using plays-within-the-play and having problems of play production serve as metaphors for more general kinds of conflict. Echegaray also shares with his fellow Nobelist the very theme of the corrosive evil of gossip, which is the subject of

Brown Brothers

*Maurice Maeterlinck of Belgium and his wife rest on their porch in California. He was granted the 1911 Nobel Prize because of his "consummate artistry, permeated with idealism."*

Pirandello's first great success, known in English as *Right You Are (If You Think You Are)*.

The modernist claims are considerably more evident for Maeterlinck, who, compared to Echegaray, was a mere boy of forty-nine when he won the Nobel in 1911. The first Nobel-winning dramatist to live more of his life in the twentieth century than the nineteenth and the first to produce any significant body of work after winning, he departed almost entirely from the traditions of the romantic and epic. He wrote, instead, assorted sym-bolist plays virtually without action, three plays for marionettes, and, most often, fairy tales. Maeterlinck plumbed what Carl Jung termed the collective unconscious—the fundamental truths of human existence that every primitive society develops myths to express. While in no way religious (he was a lifelong atheist and was buried in a civil ceremony), Maeterlinck was deeply spiritual and was generally judged by critics to have faltered in his few attempts at realism. He revived and intensified the traditions of the theater as a lyric, poetical venue rather than a quasijournalistic one, and has been an explicit or tacit influence on later playwrights, from Pirandello and Beckett to Max Frisch and Tom Stoppard.

First published as a translator of works of religious mysticism and then as an author of poems and short stories, Maeterlinck found his voice as a playwright in *The Intruder,* an 1890 depiction of a waiting family's agony as a woman suffers through, and dies after, childbirth. That austere piece was followed the same year by *The Blind,* a metaphorical glimpse of blind people trapped in a forest without a guide. The next year came the characteristically bittersweet *Seven Princesses,* in which a prince is set the task of awakening seven maidens from a sleep that will bring death. He succeeds in saving six—all but his own beloved.

While nonrealistic works are often considered difficult or challenging for ordinary audiences, Maeterlinck was genuinely popular. From early on, his plays were staged in the United States and Britain and across the Continent. Sarah Bernhardt and Mrs. Patrick Campbell starred in them; for one production, Gabriel Fauré provided incidental music. *The Blue Bird,* depicting a spiritual odyssey of two children, had its world premiere in Moscow at Stanislavski's Moscow Art Theater. Probably the best measure of Maeterlinck's artistry is that critics vary widely in judging which of his work

was best. In the Nobel presentation speech, C. D. af Wirsen of the Swedish Academy named *Aglavaine and Sélysette,* an 1896 play about a forceful woman that was one of several written by Maeterlinck to star his longtime mistress, Georgette Leblanc. *The Oxford Companion to the Theater* plumps for *The Betrothal* while also mentioning *The Burgomaster of Stilemonde.* Nowadays probably the best known are *Pélleas and Mélisande,* if primarily as the libretto for Debussy's opera about a doomed adulterous passion, and *The Blue Bird,* if mostly for the joint U.S.-Soviet film version of 1976 that starred Elizabeth Taylor and Cicely Tyson.

Maeterlinck was also an avid essayist and naturalist, using studies in the insect kingdom *(The Life of the Bee,* 1901; *The Life of the White Ant,* 1926) to illuminate human behavior. A patriotic Belgian in World War II and a dedicated antitotalitarian thereafter, he raised eyebrows in 1939 when he fled from the Nazis into the protection of the right-wing Portuguese dictator Antonio Salazar before moving on to the United States for the duration of the war.

Gerhart Hauptmann was born about three months after Maeterlinck in 1862 and like him survived through World War II. Yet some of Maeterlinck's best work and much of his world influence lay ahead of him when he received the Nobel Prize in 1911. When Hauptmann received the prize a year later—mak-

*In 1912, Gerhart Hauptmann of Germany was given the Nobel "primarily in recognition of his fruitful, varied and outstanding production in the realm of dramatic art."*

the best German-language productions (including those from Austria and Switzerland), at which stagings of his works are rarely even theoretical contenders for inclusion.

Born in Silesia, in an area now part of Poland, he grew up speaking (and later writing much of his work in) a local dialect. An indifferent and unwilling student, he was sent at age fifteen to labor for a year on an uncle's estate. There he seems to have combined the normal adolescent process of maturation with a kind of political radicalizing. "I grew conscious of myself, my value and my rights," he said three decades later. "I gained independence, firmness and a freedom of intellect that I still enjoy." He also acquired a new taste for learning and studied in succession sculpture, history, and Darwinian biology. Next came extensive readings in moderate dissidence, as exemplified by Tolstoy, Zola, and Ibsen, plus the more incendiary variety, in the works of Marx and Engels. All these studies converged in a growing commitment to a literature of social realism, which was a culturally radical step in romantic, Prussian-dominated Germany.

Hauptmann made his debut at twenty-seven at Berlin's Freie Buhne with *Before Dawn,* a fierce depiction of a peasant family's material rise and moral fall. Colloquial and dialectical, the play jolted audiences and made its author important, if controversial. His next works, *The Coming of Peace* in

ing a brief but touching speech about "the ideal of world peace, which comprehends the final ideals of art and science"—he had already done his most significant work and the play for which he was most esteemed, *The Weavers,* was already two decades behind him. He is now about as obscure as a Nobel Prize-winning writer can become—even in Germany, to judge from the documentation for the Berlin Theatertreffen, an annual festival of

1890 and *Lonely Lives* in 1891, also cut close to the bone. The latter, a portrait of marital discord, was apparently in part autobiographical. In 1893, when he was only thirty-one, Hauptmann brought forth his masterwork, *The Weavers,* which was radical in both content and form. Although nominally about a strike by Silesian workers half a century before, it was immediately recognizable as relevant to battles of the moment between capital and labor. Structurally, the play deliberately had no hero and no central story, and moved in almost documentary fashion as events dictated. The willful absence of moral preachment was, in its way, even more insurrectionist than an outright expression of sympathy for unionists would have been.

Seemingly Hauptmann himself knew he had reached a creative peak. He abruptly dropped the style that had made him famous and wrote slight comedies, including *The Beaver Coat,* about a conniving washerwoman, and strange symbolist melodramas, typified by *Hannele,* in which scenes of the brutalized life of a fourteen-year-old girl alternate with mystical passages representing her fantasies and dreams. Even when he returned to naturalism in *Florian Geyer* in 1896, he plunged into history; the play depicts the Peasants' War of 1524-25. In assessing him, the *Oxford Companion* is kinder than many other critics: "A keen eye, a feeling heart, and a creative imagination endow his charac-ters with life. In his naturalistic, and best, period, he deliberately subordinated action to circumstances, and his characters are more sinned against than sinning. In his comedies he displays human foibles with engaging benevolence, while his tragedies inspire sympathy rather than admiration."

Produced by theaters ranging from the New York Yiddish to the Bulgarian in the early years of the century, Hauptmann declined into obscurity within his lifetime. He kept writing virtually until the end of his life, but after the turn of the century about the only items of real interest that he produced were four plays written during the Nazi regime that likened the horrors of World War II to the tragic events that befell the House of Atreus in classical Greek drama. A lifelong pacifist, Hauptmann was in no way a collaborator, but he nonetheless disillusioned many admirers by remaining in Germany throughout the Hitler era. In 1945, the carpet bombing of Dresden, one of Germany's most beautiful cities and one he loved, plunged him into a deep depression, and he died of pneumonia the following year.

After the early burst of attention to playwrights, the Nobel committee waited thirteen years before honoring a dramatist again—although the delay was mitigated by the decision not to grant awards in the first and last years of World War I, 1914 and 1918, and by the choice of the poet Yeats, a some-

*In 1934, Luigi Pirandello of Italy was cited "for his bold and ingenious revival of dramatic and scenic art."*

time playwright, in 1923. When at last the Nobel committee turned to the stage, once more it chose someone whose reputation had been established in the nineteenth century. George Bernard Shaw, born in Dublin in 1856, had by 1900 brought forth *Mrs. Warren's Profession, Arms and the Man, Candida,* and *You Never Can Tell,* each of which has proved enduring enough to enjoy a major revival in New York City within the past half dozen years. Those plays alone would

ensure his reputation. The first debates the ethics of a former prostitute who worked her way out of poverty and then stayed in the business as a madam, exploiting others as she had been exploited. The second pokes fun at soldiers and the presumed glories of war and has as its hero a deserter. The third debates the distinctions between the fantasies of love and the practicalities of marriage. The last is a deft and deceptively complex send-up of the class system, in which the star part is a seemingly deferential waiter who has carefully chosen his place in the pecking order.

But the fecund Shaw kept going. By 1925, the year for which he received the Nobel (in a quirky arrangement, it was retroactively voted in 1926), he had also produced *Man and Superman, Major Barbara, Pygmalion, Heartbreak House, Back to Methuselah,* and *Saint Joan,* to name the most notable among an armada of scripts. Of these, *Saint Joan* is probably his most popular work. It vividly describes the political processes by which any true saint—which is his vision of Joan of Arc—would be found inconvenient to, and butchered by, the world's pragmatists and power brokers. Most esteemed by critics is *Heartbreak House,* in which a social gathering at a country home becomes a poignant, telling metaphor for Europe on the brink of extinction at the outbreak of World War I. A further merit of *Heartbreak House* is that, in contrast to almost all the rest of Shaw's work, it offers characters who are fully developed, recognizable human beings, rather than mere symbols or mouthpieces for points of view.

Shaw was always a tub-thumper more than an artist. He wrote innumerable books, tracts, speeches, and articles on subjects from vegetarianism to protecting your health by the choice of fabrics you wear. He could be counted on for an opinion about practically anything, asserted vehemently. In his life can be seen both the nineteenth-century ideal of the artist as a man of public values and the twentieth-century reality of the artist as media celebrity, famous above all for being famous. Shaw's crankiness extended to awards. He declined to attend the Nobel ceremony and used the money to establish a new Anglo-Swedish Literary Foundation to promote translations, especially of the work of Strindberg, who had been snubbed by his fellow Swedes on the Nobel committee. Years later, when awarded an Oscar by Hollywood for the "screenplay" of *Major Barbara,* which consisted of the dialogue from his stage play, Shaw not only refused the prize but sent a letter of righteous indignation denouncing the Motion Picture Academy's effrontery in daring to give him such a thing. While he was alive, he zealously controlled the rights to his work. Only his death made possible the most famous reuse, the stage musical and movie *My Fair Lady,*

adapted from *Pygmalion.*

Of all Nobel-winning dramatists, Shaw enjoys the greatest commercial success. In the English-speaking world, his popularity has scarcely diminished in the four decades since his death. Scarcely a season goes by without his works appearing on Broadway or in a large venue just off, and he is a staple of the regional theaters. The same is true in London and the British provinces. Canada's second largest theater is named for Shaw and produces primarily his works; the only bigger Canadian theater is devoted to Shakespeare. Shaw is produced in many languages in translation and is especially admired in Eastern Europe, where the tradition of drama as debate mirror his often didactic style.

If Shaw is the great playwright of public ideas, then Pirandello is the great playwright of inner ideas, of passion and mental turmoil. Fittingly, he was the next dramatist to win the Nobel, in 1934, barely two years before his death. Born in 1867 in Agrigento, Sicily, to a moneyed family that owned a sulphur mine, he was subjected to an arranged marriage and an enforced stint in the family business before it was recognized that he was better suited to a career as a writer and literature teacher at a women's college. In midlife, he was wounded into genius. In 1903, the family fortune was wiped out by a flood in the mine; a year after, Pirandello's wife suffered a mental breakdown from which she

*Eugene O'Neill was given the 1936 prize "for the power, honesty and deep-felt emotions of his dramatic works...."*

never recovered and for which she was institutionalized in 1919. One manifestation of her mania was wild jealousy. Although he handed over all his earnings to placate her, she continued to insist he was keeping other women.

Plunging into her deranged world, in which a veneer of logic was often wrapped around a core of hysteria, gave Pirandello the voice and subject for his greatest works, especially his 1917 play *Right You Are (If You Think You Are)*, in which confidently asserted gossip repeatedly crowds out truth, even as the author asks what right

people have to speculate about others' private lives (a dangerous question for a writer of drama or fiction, which depend on this yearning for much of their appeal). The same theme recurs in *Enrico IV* (1922), about a wealthy man who apparently believes himself to be a bygone emperor; his signature piece, *Six Characters in Search of an Author* (1921), and the closely related *Tonight We Improvise* (1930), in each of which the narrative keeps slipping from one layer of reality to another without warning; and *The Man with the Flower in His Mouth,* a brilliant one-acter pitting a jobless man, slightly deranged by cancer but touchingly aware of his life as it slips away, against a joyless and almost mute commuter, barely aware that he is alive, a format later meticulously re-created by Edward Albee in his first major play, *The Zoo Story,* and a motif and theme also explored by Thornton Wilder in *Our Town.*

Although the genesis of much of Pirandello's work was doubtless personal, some was scholarly, and a great deal was surely shaped, consciously or not, by the disillusioning experience of World War I, a war whose biggest victims were the old order and established verities. Because Pirandello's principal works emerged in the years just following, when belief was hard to come by, his vision of a universe in flux, without demonstrable truth and falsehood, quickly captivated the bourgeoisie across the Western world. Although not an original thinker on the order of Freud, Einstein, and Binet, he tapped into the same awareness of the relative, rather than invoking the nineteenth-century shibboleth of the absolute, and was treated as a major intellectual force. The extraordinary novelty of his plays wore off with the passing decades (Pirandello's reputation was also hurt by his early collaboration, later diminished, with Mussolini). But several, notably *Six Characters* and *Enrico IV,* are revived with some frequency. The latter has been performed in recent years by the film stars Richard Harris in London and Rex Harrison in New York. The former is among a cycle of Pirandello works recently adapted and staged by the noted American critic Robert Brustein for his professional troupe at Harvard University.

Eugene O'Neill, who won the Nobel Prize in 1936, was described by a wit as the only great playwright who never wrote a great play. That description would surely still apply if O'Neill were to be judged solely by the work he had produced up to the time that the Swedish Academy cited him, at age forty-eight, for "the power, honesty and deeply felt emotions of his tragic works, which embody an original concept of tragedy." Worthy as his body of work was up to that point, it did not include the three plays on which his reputation now principally rests in his homeland: *Long Day's Journey into Night,* a harrowing portrait of a day in his family's life that is generally accepted as the greatest American play and so popular that it sustained two recent Broadway productions starring, respectively, Jack Lemmon and Jason Robards just a year or so apart; *A Moon for the Misbegotten,* a sort of sequel to *Long Day's Journey,* which centers on the character representing O'Neill's brother in the years following their mother's death and was produced on Broadway about a decade ago; and *The Iceman Cometh,* a five-hour journey into the alcoholic hell of passivity and self-delusion that in recent years has enjoyed epic productions both on

*In 1957, a Broadway production of O'Neill's* Long Day's Journey into Night *starred Florence Eldridge, Bradford Dillman, Jason Robards Jr., and Fredric March.*

Broadway and in Chicago that starred, respectively, Robards and film actor Brian Dennehy. Much of O'Neill has been adapted to film and television, and even secondary works, such as *Strange Interlude* and *Marco Millions,* have enjoyed recent major productions, the former on Broadway, the latter in a coproduction between a San Francisco theater and one in China. O'Neill is also produced frequently in Britain, Scandinavia, and the rest of the world; he is especially admired in Germany, where there were half a dozen noteworthy regional productions in the 1989–90 season alone.

O'Neill was born in 1888 to the actor James O'Neill, who made his fortune touring season after season in the potboiler *The Count of Monte Cristo,* a shortsighted and self-thwarting waste of talent that became a pivotal element in the family tragedy portrayed in *Long Day's Journey.* The elder O'Neill reveled in money and attention, but his wife, who eventually became a morphine addict, and young son grew to detest the nomadic insecurity of their existence. For three years, from the age of seven to ten, Eugene lived in a boarding school. When he returned home, it was to a mother irredeemably

23

hooked. Although the rest of the family alternately pitied and scorned her affliction, as is evident in *Long Day's Journey,* Eugene and his guiding older brother, Jamie, were at least as dissolute. Boozing and whoring got Eugene ousted from Princeton University before he completed a single year. Soon after, he married impulsively, fathered a son, and then abandoned bride and child for an eighteen-month trip around the world, much of it spent as a deckhand or derelict. This dissipation became the basis for the best of O'Neill's art. The bar where he rotted, Jimmy the Priest's, served as the model for Harry Hope's saloon in *Iceman.* The roistering with his brother, the aimless wandering, the tuberculosis he contracted, and even his writer's despondency at just not being good enough to express what he saw all reappeared in *Long Day's Journey,* a play so personal that O'Neill suppressed it for the last dozen years of his life. It was produced at his wife's behest a couple of years after his death, despite his apparent instructions to withhold it even longer.

Before these unforgettable personal plays, however, came a whole stream of more detached experiments, from the sea drama *Bound East for Cardiff* to the fraternal struggle *Beyond the Horizon,* which won him the first of four Pulitzer Prizes in drama. (The others in his lifetime were for *Anna Christie,* a seafaring tale whose title character is a prostitute, and *Strange Interlude,* a formal experiment in using the old tradition of the aside, or remark to the audience, as a means for characters to voice their innermost thoughts in stream of consciousness. He was awarded a fourth posthumously for *Long Day's Journey.)* The roster of O'Neill plays includes *Desire Under the Elms,* an almost Gothic tale of adultery and incest set in New England; *Mourning Becomes Electra,* an adaptation of the *Oresteia* of Aeschylus, set during the American Civil War; *The Emperor Jones,* a portrait of a murderous Pullman car porter who becomes ruler of a West Indian island, which for its time was considered a daringly sympathetic use of black acting talent; and his only comedy, *Ah, Wilderness!,* a nostalgic glimpse of a bourgeois Fourth of July at the turn of the century. The last demonstrated that O'Neill, the American theater's most prolific experimenter in form and style, could have been the foremost boulevardier of his time, had he wished. Within the past half dozen years both the play and its musical adaptation, *Take Me Along,* have been revived on Broadway.

After O'Neill the Swedish Academy waited thirty-three years before honoring another playwright, and then it chose a man also distinguished for fiction. Samuel Barclay Beckett, who received the award in 1969, at sixty-three, and who lived on another twenty years, was at once the most singular and the most characteristic voice of

Bettmar/Hulton

*Samuel Beckett of Ireland won the 1969 Nobel "for his writing, which—in new forms for the novel and drama— in the destitution of modern man acquires its elevation."*

into the exploration of nothingness. None was more persistent, more haunted by war and holocaust, nuclear threat and nihilism, depression and paranoia and pointless pain, than Beckett. The Irish-born minimalist of *Waiting for Godot, Endgame,* and *Krapp's Last Tape* and of the novels *Molloy, Malone Dies* and *The Unnamable* simply distilled despair. Beckett's works were often funny—the two battered tramps of *Godot* might have been written for Laurel and Hardy and were in fact played by the film stars Bert Lahr and Tom Ewell, and later by Robin Williams and Steve Martin—but the humor intensified the sadness. In that play's most vivid and haunting image, one character cries out about all mankind, "They give birth astride of a grave." Beckett regarded himself as less an artist than a historian, a sort of chronicler of misbegotten times. "I didn't invent this buzzing confusion," he said. "It's all around us and the only chance of renewal is to open our eyes and see the mess."

Born on a disputed date in 1906 (characteristically, he also had his death kept secret until after his funeral), Beckett claimed to remember being a fetus in the womb, a place he recalled not as a haven but as a dark ocean of agony. After literary studies, he went to Paris and fell in with James Joyce, whom he regarded as a friend and inspiration—although, as Beckett later noted, Joyce tended toward omniscience and omnipotence in his narra-

the twentieth century.

The most evident social trend of this century has been consolidation—multinational businesses, globalized politics, homogenized cultures. Amid this bustling bigness and togetherness has been heard a persistent cry of smallness and aloneness, a sense that each individual has been left isolated with nameless terrors, deterioration, and death. Many of the century's most imaginative artists poured their being

tive voice, "whereas I work with impotence and ignorance." After an abortive return to Dublin, Beckett was back living in Paris again in 1939 when the Nazis invaded, and he and his wife fled to the free south of France, traveling by night and hiding by day. That footsore journey probably inspired the futile wandering in *Godot,* according to its first Broadway director, Beckett's friend Alan Schneider. An even deeper real-life influence in Beckett's work, scholars have suggested, came in 1938. As Beckett walked along a Paris street, a panhandler stabbed him in the chest, perforating a lung and narrowly missing his heart. When Beckett later asked why the attack happened, the assailant replied, "I don't know, sir," a phrase that appears verbatim at a pivotal point in *Godot.*

While building up the experiences that would make him famous, Beckett labored in obscurity until the spectacular burst from 1951 to 1953, when *Godot* and three novels appeared to acclaim. By 1960 he had added *Endgame,* a vision of the end of the world; *Happy Days,* the foremost of a series of plays in which the dominant metaphor is physical frustration (in this case, a character is buried in sand); and *Krapp's Last Tape,* a long one-act monologue in which speech has broken down into elliptical phrases, presaging a series of shorter plays that were virtually or entirely wordless. Thereafter, Beckett's writings became fewer and fewer, shorter and shorter,

bleaker and bleaker. But he never quite lapsed into the ultimate artistic despair of silence. His last work, *Stirrings Still,* a piece of fewer than two thousand words (the exact number of words, and the metaphoric reasons for the number, became a matter of lively scholarly debate), was published in March 1989, in an edition limited to two hundred copies. His vision never yielded. Even on a sunny day in London, as he strolled through a park in evident pleasure, when a friend remarked that it was a day to make one glad to be alive, Beckett turned and said, "I wouldn't go that far."

The first African writer to win the Nobel Prize was, fittingly, a man who blended the Western traditions that the Swedish Academy had been accustomed to honoring with literary traditions drawn from the tribal tale-telling of his own people. Akinwande Oluwole Babtunde Soyinka was born in 1934 into the Yoruba tribe, the middle class (his father was an Anglican school headmaster), and the British empire, in what later became independent Nigeria. While still in his teens, he was writing plays and short stories that were broadcast on the radio. He studied at the university level both in his homeland and in Leeds, England, where he earned a B.A. and wrote his first two plays of consequence, *The Swamp Dwellers* and *The Lion and the Jewel,* which defined what has remained his principal theme, the un-

Nigeria's Wole Soyinka received the 1986 prize because of the poetic overtones with which he fashions "the drama of existence."

dence approached, he returned home to University College, Ibadan, in 1960. Within a few months he mounted the elaborate play *A Dance of the Forests* as part of that year's independence ceremonies and also the satire *The Trials of Brother Jero,* which is still produced in the West. He was soon writing for a weekly series on radio and television and lecturing at a university.

But he just as quickly began to clash with established political and cultural authority. His cultural sin was an attack on "negritude," an anti-Western, antiassimilationist concept that was rooted, as he saw it, in xenophobia and mistrust of progress. To him, such rhetoric too often served as a substitute for the harder business of amelioration and reform. Said Soyinka, "A tiger does not shout its tigritude. It acts." Soyinka compounded the antagonism by writing most of his works in English, the language of the former oppressor but also the only one that gave him a chance at an international audience; only his poems are written in Yoruba.

Politically, his crime was bolder still. He resigned from the faculty at the University of Ife in 1963 rather than obey a government directive that all faculty members support the legitimacy of the ruling authorities, and a couple of years later Soyinka was jailed for allegedly staging an anonymous broadcast asserting that regional elections had been rigged. International

easy relationship between Western-influenced progress and Africa's village-based tradition—a conflict about which the author's own feelings seem to be split. Taken up by London's ardently political Royal Court Theatre, Soyinka temporarily abandoned the scholarly life to work as a scrutinizer of scripts and a director of student actors, primarily in his own work, including an antiracist play called *The Invention.* But as Nigerian indepen-

protest secured his relief, but his position remained shaky. It cannot have been helped by the 1965 publication of his best prose work, *The Interpreters,* a novel about five young intellectuals recently returned from the United States and Europe to a Nigeria that they regard as rotten.

Two years later, Soyinka again plunged into politics, this time meeting secretly with an Ibo tribal leader— in his version, to dissuade the group from secession, but in the government's version, to conspire at rebellion. For twenty-seven months he was confined alone in a cell four feet by eight feet without human contact, books, writing implements, or medical care, in fear for his life. Although he was released in 1969, he went into voluntary exile the following year and returned only after a coup in 1975. Even then, he did not receive a universal hero's welcome. Although distinctly African by the standards of most Western artists and critics, he remains too European in the eyes of many of his countrymen.

In awarding him the Nobel Prize primarily for his drama—although he is also esteemed for his poetry, his fiction, and an autobiography, *Ake, the Years of Childhood*—Lars Gyllensten of the Swedish Academy said, "[Soyinka's] plays make frequent and skillful use of many elements belonging to stage art which also have genuine roots in African culture—dance and rites, masques and pantomime, rhythm and music,

declamation, theater within the theater. The myths, traditions and rites are integrated as nourishment for his writing, not a masquerade costume." This characteristic amalgam of East and West, or rather North and South, can be seen especially clearly in Soyinka's best-known play, *Death and the King's Horseman,* a sprawling political drama that has been mounted in recent years in both London and New York (it had its U.S. premiere in a 1979 Chicago production directed by the author). Henry Louis Gates Jr., Soyinka's biographer and the foremost United States scholar of Afro-American literature, says in a controversial assertion of cross-cultural equality, "Soyinka's texts are superbly realized, complex mediations between the European dramatic tradition and the equally splendid Yoruba dramatic tradition. This form of verbal expression, uniquely his own, he uses to address the profoundest matters of human moral order and cosmic will."

Most Western critics are not, in truth, as enthusiastic as Gates or the Swedish Academy. But most are also not versed in the African half of Soyinka's dramatic vocabulary. Many would dispute whether the Yoruba tradition is as splendid as the Western European. Yet it is a striking if sobering thought that the only dramatists to receive the Nobel Prize in more than half a century are a man who largely lost faith in words as a means of dramatic expression and a man who remains incom-

Death and the King's Horseman *was given an elaborate production. Soyinka himself directed a 1979 Chicago version of the play.*

pletely reconciled to the stage traditions of the West. Perhaps the drama needs some reinventing—if not in Soyinka's fashion, then in someone's—to reclaim its former eminence in the literature of the world. ■

*Nobel Prize laureates Kendall, Friedman, and Taylor paused on their way to a Stockholm television interview.*

# CHAPTER 2

# THE NOBEL PRIZE IN PHYSICS

## THE WORK OF PROFESSOR JEROME I. FRIEDMAN, PROFESSOR HENRY W. KENDALL, PROFESSOR RICHARD E. TAYLOR

*This year's laureates and their coworkers examined the proton (and later on also the neutron) under a microscope—not an ordinary one, but a two-mile-long electron accelerator at Stanford, California. A totally new facet of proton behavior was displayed. A new rung on the ladder of creation had revealed itself, and a new epic in the history of physics had begun.*
*—Professor Cecilia Jarlskog, member*
*of the Royal Swedish Academy of*
*Sciences and member of the Nobel*
*Committee for Physics*

*Three quarks for Muster Mark!*
*Sure he hasn't got much of a bark.*
*And sure any he has it's all beside*
*the mark.*

To some literary scholars, the "quarks" that James Joyce had in mind when he wrote this passage in *Finnegans Wake* were Bronx cheers for the unfortunate cuckolded King Mark of the Tristan legend. To others, it was a play on "quarts," an order for a hefty portion of Irish ale. In German, *Quark* is a kind of runny cheese. But to theoretical physicist Murray Gell-Mann of the California Insti-

tute of Technology, "quarks" were just what the subatomic fraternity was looking for. He was toying with the notion that the protons and neutrons that form atomic nuclei might not be the indivisible entities that physicists believed, but might instead be formed of smaller bits—which he dubbed "quarks." It seemed somehow appropriate, Gell-Mann says in the excellent account of twentieth-century physics by Robert Crease and Charles Mann entitled *The Second Creation:* "A strange sound for something peculiar." Later, as Gell-Mann was preparing to write up his thoughts, he was leafing through *Finnegans Wake*

*Friedman says, "Teaching is a very important part of my life."*

when he came across the Muster Mark doggerel. "That's it!" he burst out, for in his scheme, three quarks made a neutron or a proton.

Unfortunately, Gell-Mann's quarks had the annoying property of not being easily observed. That was too bad, for quarks otherwise had a lot going for them. The early 1960s were a time of frustration and even boredom in high-energy physics, the study of particles smaller than an atomic nucleus. Whiz-bang particle accelerators— "atom smashers" to the headline writers—

were blasting protons and neutrons and netting a veritable zoo of "fundamental particles," given names like "kaons" and "pions," "sigmas" and "lambdas." There were so many new particles that physicists were in danger of running out of Greek letters to name them all.

It was the wisdom of Gell-Mann and George Zweig, another Caltech physicist who independently proposed the existence of quarks in 1964, to make sense of the particle proliferation by suggesting that they could all be formed out of triplets or quark-anti-quark pairs. But quarks remained little more than mathematical entities, a classification scheme to bring order to the Greek zoo. Certainly not the humdrum experiment being proposed by a group including Richard E. Taylor of the Stanford Linear Accelerator Center (SLAC) and Henry W. Kendall and Jerome I. Friedman of the Massachusetts Institute of Technology, winners of the 1990 Nobel Prize in physics for the results of that seemingly unpromising experiment.

The three had met during the 1950s. Taylor was a graduate student doing research in the physics department. Kendall and Friedman were postdoctoral fellows at Stanford University's High-Energy Physics Lab. Friedman and Kendall worked in Robert Hofstadter's group and spent the decade shooting electrons at nuclei of all sorts of atoms, from hydrogen to lead. He showed that protons and neutrons are diffuse blobs about one-ten-trillionth of a centimeter across. For measuring the size and shape of protons, Hofstadter won the Nobel Prize in physics in 1961. When

*Jerome I. Friedman accepted the Nobel Prize medal and diploma from King Carl XVI Gustaf.*

*Kendall says, "I think many scientists start very, very young."*

Taylor, Friedman, and Kendall joined forces in 1964, they simply wanted to get a clearer picture of these nuclear fuzzballs. Their experiment was akin to building a camera to take a sharper picture of Mars—and then spying canals through the viewfinder.

The trio's talents complemented each other perfectly. Taylor, tall and flamboyant, is an experimentalist's experimentalist, a meticulous detail man who leaves nothing to chance. He grew up in a small town on Canada's western prairie; the only

child of a teacher and a representative of a flour milling firm who traveled almost constantly, he recalls that his mother "could devote her full attention to me five days a week." The isolation of the prairie bred "a drive, a wanting to understand the world," he recalls. Taylor got his master of science degree at the University of Alberta and then went to Stanford for graduate work.

Kendall, from patrician Yankee stock, has been described as an electronics genius second to none. He thinks that he was only "five or six" when he developed an interest in things mechanical and technical that "just grew" into an interest in physics. After studying mathematics at Amherst College, Kendall received his doctorate from MIT in 1955 and joined its faculty in 1961. Eight years later, he helped found the Union of Concerned Scientists, which has studied and lobbied on issues of arms control, the Strategic Defense Initiative ("Star Wars"), and nuclear power; he has been chairman of the group since 1973. An avid mountaineer, he likes "to go where no human being has been before. I have done that in physics."

Friedman, on the MIT faculty since 1960 and the William A. Coolidge Professor of Physics since 1988, is described by colleagues as determined, solid—and brilliant. His wife calls him "very down-to-earth" and able to explain anything clearly without talking down. As a child, he was more artist than scientist, spending several hours a day painting in the art school within his Chicago high school. "I thought I would end up being a painter," he recalls. He won scholarships to both the Universi-

*Henry W. Kendall sat in the Nobel Foundation's board room, where medals and certificates were displayed.*

*Taylor says, "The design of an experiment can be full of joy."*

ty of Chicago and the Art Institute of Chicago. After much soul-searching, he opted for the university. In high school, he had read a little tome by Albert Einstein, *The Meaning of Relativity.* "I never really understood it conceptually [but] felt that sometime in my life I wanted to understand." And that meant continuing his education, relegating painting to Sundays. Friedman spent summers operating the university's cyclotron, an early accelerator, and earned his doctorate from the university in 1956.

When he, Taylor, and Kendall got together they had no intention of looking for quarks. They were just going to bring into sharper focus Hofstadter's picture of the proton. "When we started, people thought it was a dead-end research project," says Friedman. "We didn't know what we were looking for. But it was so exciting. We were all very young. They said, 'Here, take this wonderful machine and do something great with it.'" Taylor says, "We were raising the energy and were quite excited about it."

That beautiful machine was SLAC, begun in 1962 and switched on in 1967. Twenty-five feet below the surface, the particle accelerator tunnels for two miles under the orchards and interstate highway of the Santa Clara Valley in California. At one end, a strong electrical field rips the electrons off the atoms making up a piece of hot metal oxide. They immediately enter the accelerator, where they are sped up by high-power microwaves until they are hurtling along at almost the speed of light. They reach the end of the tunnel in about a hundred-thousandth of a second. For their experiment, the MIT-SLAC team shot SLAC's electrons into a tank of liquid hydrogen or heavy hydrogen; the former contains only protons in the nuclei and the latter, neutrons as well as protons. The idea was to see how the electrons bounced off the nuclei, as Hofstadter had done for a decade. For that reason, some physicists regarded the experiment as derivative, unoriginal, and basically a waste of precious accelerator time.

*Richard Taylor escorted Marion Peterson, wife of the speaker of Parliament, down the grand staircase of the Blue Hall to the Nobel banquet.*

## SCIENCE AND ART
### (Interview)

**I** went to a high school on the West Side of Chicago, and I spent about three years as an art student. I spent two or three hours a day in art school, painting and learning about art. There was a time when I thought I would end up being a painter. In fact, when I graduated from high school, I had a scholarship to the Art Institute of Chicago Art School, and I also had a scholarship to the University of Chicago at that point.

"I did a lot of soul-searching, and I realized that I really wanted to further my academic education, so I took the scholarship to the University of Chicago. The college there was very unusual, with a special education program set up by Robert Maynard Hutchins. Everything was the original writings of the great thinkers. It was a wonderful experience. . . .

"Physics has an enormous amount of creativity in it—just like art—and there is also a very important concept of aesthetics. Frequently you will see people develop a series of equations, and the phrase will be used 'that this is a beautiful set of equations.' What does that mean? It means that somehow these equations embody the content of the system that's being described in a very elegant way. So elegance and beauty are really important as a sort of underlying point of view in science."—Jerome I. Friedman

For the first half of 1967, the team measured "elastic" collisions between electrons and protons: The protons remained unchanged during the interaction, the electrons bouncing off them like billiard balls. The collisions produced what everyone expected. Just as Hofstadter had found, the protons behaved as Jell-O would if bombarded with grapes or, according to Taylor, the way a cloud would if hit with raindrops: They could not deflect the electrons much at all. The proton seemed to be a smooth, structureless distribution of charge.

During the second half of 1967 the MIT-SLAC group finished elastic scattering and then measured "inelastic scattering." In this type of interaction, the electrons hit protons with enough fury to smash them to smithereens. The physicists started to analyze the scattered electron data in 1968. It was messy, for the smashed protons had left in their wake the complex debris of other particles—producing a confusing array of electrons. The trio could tell that they were not seeing what everyone had predicted. The smart money said that the electrons should ricochet off the protons mostly at small angles, just as in elastic scattering. Taylor, Friedman, and Kendall found instead that many were careening off to the side a hundred times more frequently than anyone had expected. Someone had put grape seeds in the Jell-O or hail in the cloud. After searching for possible errors and finding none, "we knew there was something very unusual happening," recalls Friedman. "But we didn't know what."

The findings echoed a historic moment. In the first decade of this century, Ernest Rutherford shot alpha particles (helium nuclei) at a thin sheet of gold foil. The alpha particles scattered to the side much more often than one would have thought, given that the atomic nuclei of gold (and every other sort of atom) were thought to be diffuse mushballs. In 1911 this "wide-angle scattering" showed instead that nuclei consist of concentrations of mass and charge.

Could protons and neutrons also have such concentrations? Theoretical physicists tried to make sense of the results, but SLAC's James Bjorken had come up with complicated predictions that only a few physicists could fully understand. When Caltech physicist Richard Feynmann visited SLAC and saw the data, he came back the next day and said the results fit his notion that protons and neutrons were made of things called partons. Recalled Kendall in *The Second Creation,* "Feynmann being Feynmann, if Feynmann says that you fellows are observing pointlike constituents in the nucleon, then you pay attention."

They did. Combined with Bjorken's theory, their data began to make sense. If there are small electrically charged kernels within a proton, to an electron which didn't disrupt the proton they would look like a smooth, spread-out charge. But to a speeding electron, the kernels would seem to be almost stationary, because when an object moves at nearly the speed of light, time slows down, which is analogous to movement slowing.

## EXPLORING
(Interview)

**I** like to go where no human being has been before. I have done that in physics, done it a number of times with colleagues. We sometimes find things, and sometimes we do not. But it is extraordinarily interesting.

"I like to go in the mountains to places where no one has been before. The world is an astonishingly beautiful place. It's beautiful at the deep level of physics, way down inside things. What we know of the universe that's visible to us is of astonishing beauty, and I like to see that and to explore it. That's why I take photographs. That's why I engage in research. It's a great privilege to be able to carry out researches and to have access to the great facilities that make these studies possible.

"I have always liked the mountains and the sea and the Arctic, which I have visited only recently. I think these are places of great beauty. These can be appreciated on a large scale in quite striking contrast to the microscopic things that I study professionally. I carry a large camera. I have been to the high mountains; I take photographs underwater. What I find enriches my life."—Henry Kendall

## GROWING UP
### (Interview)

**I** come from a very small town on the Canadian prairies. In those towns, there are often families that are not particularly rich, but they think of themselves as belonging. I was an only child in my family, but I lived in an extended family. . . .

"We must have had good teachers. There are an enormous number of people from that town that have done well. Partly it's the drive that you get from feeling isolated and wanting to understand the world.

"My father was probably fairly clever, but he went to World War I at sixteen or seventeen and was shot up fairly badly. I think he had planned to go into pharmacy as a young boy, but he did not go back to school after the war.

"My mother was a schoolteacher, and during my early life my father used to travel around Alberta for the flour milling company. Flour milling was one of the major industries in our little town. And so my mother could devote her full attention to me five days a week. I'm told that's something that's quite common to successful people—their mothers told them they were something special."—Richard Taylor

But this realization took time. Kendall says, "It was not like Archimedes discovering the law of buoyancy and jumping out of his bathtub shouting, 'Eureka!'" To the contrary, they checked and rechecked the experiment into the l970s. And when they concluded that the proton indeed contained discrete pointlike granules—what Friedman calls "little hard nuggets of matter" and Kendall likens to "rocks in a bale of cotton"—few realized how fundamental the discovery was. "It took nearly ten years before the complete consequences of this experiment rolled out," says Kendall. Friedman adds, "The idea of quarks as real physical entities was objected to as totally unreasonable. Old physics dies with great difficulty."

But die it did. The MIT-SLAC collaboration proved the physical reality of quarks—a finding so important that many observers of physics wonder why the Nobel Committee took so long to recognize the achievement. By the mid-l970s, quarks were accepted as real particles, not mathematical abstractions. The quark model is now the centerpiece of the standard model of subatomic physics. In the years since the discovery, physicists have identified five "flavors" of the pointlike particles. In keeping with Gell-Mann's whimsy, the quarks have been dubbed "up," "down," "strange," "charm," and "bottom" (or "beauty"). They carry fractions of the proton's charge—plus or minus one-third or two-thirds. A neutron is made of two down quarks and one up quark; a proton, of two ups and one down. Because there are six members of the other

*Taylor, Friedman and Kendall were interviewed before a television taping in Stockholm.*

group of basic particles, which includes the electron, physicists (who worship symmetry) believe that there are six quarks too. The missing one, for which the search is on, has been dubbed "top," or "truth."

And if truth is found, what next? Kendall and Friedman are turning their efforts to help develop a particle detector for the superconducting super collider (SSC), which would be the most powerful accelerator ever. "With the SSC," says Friedman, "we may find a level of structure lying within quarks themselves." Taylor is part of a team of physicists conducting experiments at a machine in Germany that smashes a beam of protons and a beam of electrons. He, too, can imagine glimpsing something smaller than a quark. It would not be the first time that physicists had found that particles thought to be indivisible had smaller constituents after all.  ■

*Nobel Prize laureate Elias J. Corey says, "Of all the pleasures in life, there is nothing quite the same as sitting by myself in my study with a complicated problem . . . ."*

# CHAPTER 3

# THE NOBEL PRIZE IN CHEMISTRY

## THE WORK OF PROFESSOR ELIAS J. COREY

*Organic synthesis—the production of complicated compounds, using simple and cheap starting materials—is one of the prerequisites of our civilization, the chemical age in which we live. This year's Nobel laureate has made extremely important contributions in this area.*
*—Professor Salo Gronowitz, member*
*of the Royal Swedish Academy of*
*Sciences and Chairman of the Nobel*
*Committee for Chemistry*

Elias J. Corey has mastered the art of making something valuable from almost nothing. This may sound like flimflam, but in his Harvard laboratory, he assembles molecular bits and pieces—almost nothing—into an array of valuables, transmuting the body's own regulators into pharmaceuticals that can save lives.

His great invention is a technique for finding, among millions of possibilities, the simplest steps for assembling complex organic molecules. "It's a logical method for finding needles in haystacks," says Corey. Obtaining organic molecules in quantity directly from nature can be costly or even impossible, since they often are produced in tiny quantities. Our bodies, for instance, manufacture physiologically powerful hormones, such as prostaglan-

dins, only a few molecules at a time.

How to synthesize such rare organic compounds in the laboratory has long preoccupied chemists. The Royal Swedish Academy of Sciences noted in awarding Corey the 1990 Nobel Prize in chemistry, "Organic synthesis, that is, the production of complicated organic compounds using simple and cheap starting material, is one of the prerequisites of our civilization."

In 1902 the second Nobel Prize in chemistry ever awarded went to Emil Fischer for his synthesis of sugars and purines. In 1905, Adolf von Baeyer won for work on organic dyes. Since then, five additional Nobel Prizes in chemistry have been awarded for work on synthesis. In some ways, however, those earlier achievements, although science, smacked of art. "Many earlier syntheses were performed more or less intuitively, so that their planning was difficult to conceive," the Swedish Royal Academy noted in summing up Corey's achievements. "Asking a chemist how he came upon precisely the starting materials and reactions that so elegantly led to the desired result would probably be as meaningless as asking Picasso why he painted as he did." As a result, chemists could not fully exploit the potential for mass-producing complex natural compounds in the laboratory.

Elias J. Corey's insight was to attack the problem of synthesizing molecules the way a precocious child attacks the problem of finding out what makes a clock tick. The child's strategy is to disassemble the clock. If truly precocious, the child will note which gear connects to which spring. Then he will be able to reassemble the clock as it was. And if the child could find similar springs and gears on sale for a few cents at the hardware store, he could build his own clock at minimal cost.

Of course, molecules are more complex than any clock. "The process of synthetic planning has been likened to a game of three-dimensional chess using 40 pieces at each side," said the Swedish Royal Academy. The complexity comes about because a particular organic molecule may contain scores of atoms of carbon, hydrogen, oxygen, and other elements bonded into a unique three-dimensional shape.

"Retrosynthetic analysis," as Corey calls the technique that earned him the Nobel Prize, begins with the natural molecule. First, the chemist analyzes the structure of the molecule to be reproduced. Next,

instead of guessing what compounds might be fitted together to synthesize this "target compound," the chemist approaches it as the child did the clock. Beginning in the 196Os, Corey established rules for dissecting such a molecule: Breaking the chemical bonds that hold it together reduces a molecule to its major building blocks, which can in turn be broken apart in the same way. The chemist winds up with simple compounds figuratively spread out on the lab table. Since these simple compounds are readily available and cost little, the chemist can now amass the raw materials and fit them together, inexpensively synthesizing the target molecule in quantity.

"There is not a pharmaceutical laboratory in the world that does not use products from our work," Corey has said. "And by 'our' I mean not just me but the hundreds of colleagues, postdoctoral fellows, and graduate students who have helped me."

Chemistry was not Corey's first interest. As a child, he preferred football and baseball. He was born in 1928, in Methuen, Massachusetts, the grandson of Lebanese immigrants. When he was eighteen months old, his father died. His mother then changed her youngest child's name from William to his father's name, Elias. "I have always been guided by a desire to be a worthy son to the father I do not remember and to the loving, courageous mother who raised me, my brother, and my two sisters," Corey says.

His mother's sister and her husband moved in with the Coreys, creating an extended family that got through the de-

*His name called, Corey stood in preparation for accepting his award.*

## THE JOYS OF TEACHING
### (Interview)

Those students whom I taught in the sixties and the seventies are now leaders in the field. They are part of the Corey family. There are really two scientific or professional families: There is the group of students whom I have taught in lecturing in formal courses, who have not been members of my research group, and then there are the others, who have worked directly with me in research. It is this second group which I regard as the Corey research family. Altogether, there are more than 400 individuals who have worked as members of my research group over the years.

"Of that number, about 150 hold academic professorships—all around the world in many different countries. I visit them quite regularly, and we often have large convocations of the local family. This year, I visited India and met with about twenty former coworkers. I visited France and met with about fifteen coworkers from that country, and later I went to Korea, where I have more than sixty former students who are very active in academic work and in the pharmaceutical industry. In the summer, I visited Japan, and there was a meeting of more than sixty of my former coworkers who are active as professors or research directors in the pharmaceutical industry of Japan.

"It is very satisfying to have had a part in the education of so many individuals who are now leaders in the field of chemistry all over the world. I find that I derive as much satisfaction from following the discoveries of my students as I do from my own work."—Elias J. Corey

pression of the 193Os by working hard. At a Catholic elementary school, Corey developed a liking for Latin and mathematics. In 1945, after graduating from high school at age sixteen, he enrolled at the Massachusetts Institute of Technology. He had been warned that he would be unable to earn a living as a mathematician, and so he took a range of courses to discover what might interest him. It turned out to be organic chemistry. The reason, he says, was organic chemistry's "intrinsic beauty and its great relevance to human health."

Corey graduated after three years and then worked on the synthesis of penicillin as an MIT graduate student. The University of Illinois offered him a lectureship but stipulated that he be ready in six weeks. Corey stopped all research to write his thesis, completing it in just four weeks. In January 1951 he took up his new post. It was a teaching position, and so for the next three years he had to conduct research on his own. Meanwhile, he had grown dissatisfied with the way synthetic chemistry was being taught, case by case, as if each molecule to be synthesized were a separate riddle that must be solved in its own way. He committed himself to discovering underlying principles of chemical synthesis.

In 1959, Corey joined the faculty at Harvard University. His uncle, whom he regarded as a second father, had recently died. "In solitude and sadness," he buried himself in his research. He began working out his new approach to synthesis, breaking the target molecule into ever smaller components until he arrived at building

*Corey's companion at the formal banquet was Queen Sylvia.*

blocks that were both simple and commercially available. Logical as it was, his technique at first drew skepticism—and even ridicule—from colleagues, who believed that no single system could apply to all natural organic molecules because they are so varied and complex. As Corey puts it, he was developing unified rules for "a zoo of chemical structures." But he serenely worked on, developing retrosynthetic analysis into a powerful tool, today widely used.

By the mid-1960s, working with graduate students, he was beginning to harness computer graphics to retrosynthetic analysis. Since then, Corey and his collabora-

tors have produced a program, LHASA, that allows a chemist, using a magnetic stylus, mouse, or light pen, to draw the target molecule in a form the computer can "see." Working with the program, which includes a data base containing more than two thousand known chemical reactions, the chemist can partially automate the task of retrosynthetically dissecting the target molecule into building blocks that can be manipulated. Today, many chemists use such programs to help devise simple sequences of steps for synthesizing a desired molecule.

In his Harvard laboratory, where Corey developed the retrosynthetic technique,

## COREY'S ORGANIC SYNTHESIS
### by Professor Salo Gronowitz (Excerpts)

The synthesis of complicated organic compounds often shows elements of artistic creation. Many earlier syntheses were performed more or less intuitively, so that their planning was difficult to perceive. Asking a chemist why he chose precisely the starting materials and reactions that so elegantly led to the desired result would probably be as meaningless as asking Picasso why he painted as he did.

The process of synthetic planning has been compared to a game of three-dimensional chess using forty pieces on each side. But the problem of synthesis may be even harder than this. Over 35,000 usable methods of synthesis are described in the chemical literature, each with its possibilities and its limitations. During synthesis, moreover, new methods appear which can modify the strategy. It is like allowing new moves during a game of chess.

Beginning in the 1960s Professor E. J. Corey coined the term and developed the concept of retrosynthetic analysis. Starting from the structure of the molecule he was to produce, the target molecule, he established rules for how it should be dissected into smaller parts, and what strategic bonds should be broken. In this way, less complicated building blocks were obtained, which could later be assembled in the process of synthesis. These building blocks were then analyzed in the same way until simple compounds had been reached, whose synthesis was already described in the literature or which were commercially available. Corey showed that strict logical retrosynthetic analysis was amenable to computer programming. He is the leader of this rapidly developing field.

Through his brilliant analysis of the theory of organic synthesis, Corey has been able to carry out total syntheses of around a hundred naturally occurring biologically active compounds, according to simple logical principles, which previously was very difficult to achieve. Only a few of his achievements in organic synthesis can be mentioned here. In 1978 he prepared gibberellic acid, which belongs to a class of very important plant hormones of complicated structure. Corey has furthermore synthesized gingkolide B, which is the active substance in an extract from the ginkgo tree and is used as a folk medicine in China.

Corey's most important syntheses are concerned with prostaglandins and related compounds. These often very unstable compounds are responsible for multifarious and vital regulatory functions of significance in reproduction, blood coagulation and normal and pathological processes in the immune system. Their importance is witnessed by the awarding of the 1982 Nobel Prize in physiology or medicine to Professors Sune Bergström, Bengt Samuelsson and Sir John Vane for their discovery of prostaglandins and closely related biologically active compounds.

With enormous skill Corey has carried out the total syntheses of a large number of such compounds. It is thanks to Corey's contributions that many of these important pharmaceuticals are commercially available.

To perform these total syntheses successfully, Corey was also obliged to develop some fifty entirely new or considerably improved synthesis reactions. His systematic use of different types of organometallic reagents has revolutionized recent techniques of synthesis in many respects. In recent years he has also introduced a number of very effective enzyme-like catalysts, which yield only one mirror isomer of the target product in certain types of synthetically important reactions. No other chemist has developed such a comprehensive and varied assortment of methods often showing the simplicity of genius, which have become commonplace in organic synthesis laboratories. ■

*Corey took to the podium to deliver his remarks.*

he and his colleagues have put it to work, synthesizing important organic compounds. For instance, in the 1960s Corey focused on prostaglandins, a group of hormones still incompletely understood.

Prostaglandins are essential in regulating everything from muscle contractions to blood pressure. Yet, our bodies produce them in such minute quantities that they were virtually mystery compounds when Corey began his work. Corey says, "The first synthesis was done with practically no knowledge of the chemical properties of these compounds; such small quantities had been available that there was very little information in the literature."

Nevertheless, by 1968 he had completed the first synthesis of a prostaglandin, and by the next year, "the synthesis of all the prostaglandins and countless analogues was for the first time possible on any scale." Throughout the 1970s and the 1980s, Corey's group continued to study these compounds, developing new methods for synthesizing them. The Royal Swedish Academy noted, "It is thanks to Corey's contributions that many of these important pharmaceuticals are commercially available."

Corey has synthesized a hundred or so additional molecules, including ginkgolide B. Since ancient times an extract of

## WHY BUILD MOLECULES?
(Interview)

In the twentieth century, medicine has made tremendous advances. For many illnesses, a physician can prescribe a medicine to treat that illness. Almost all of those medicines are composed of synthetic compounds made by chemists and made in chemical factories for pharmaceutical factories.

"Most of medicine today is dependent on synthetic, organic compounds because these are very special substances that function to change the course of a disease. Antibiotics are used to treat infection. Most antibiotics which are in use now are synthetic. They are made not by nature but by humans. They are man-made compounds, and chemical synthesis is involved in every step of the development of those therapeutic agents.

"In the beginning of a research project, molecules are synthesized according to some theory or idea that they might have an appropriate biological activity—for instance, to kill certain microorganisms. They are tested, and if they do have that biological activity, then those molecules are selected for clinical studies and large-scale manufacture. At almost every step in that process, synthetic chemistry is essential.

"Synthetic chemistry is really the heart of chemistry, and chemistry, especially the chemistry of carbon compounds or the family of carbon compounds, is the basic language of all life."—Elias J. Corey

leaves of the ginkgo tree has been used as a folk medicine in China. Today, sales of the natural extract total approximately $500 million annually. It is used to treat circulatory disturbances in the elderly and asthma. The tree itself is extinct in the wild, but it was preserved by Buddhist monks in Japan and China, who considered ginkgos sacred and planted them outside their temples. The active molecule in the extract, ginkgolide B, is extremely complicated and daunting to synthesize. However, Corey synthesized it in 1988, in twenty-four steps.

"Teaching is as important to me as research," Corey says. "I still teach first-year graduate students, and I do whatever I can, whenever I can, to get young people excited about science and mathematics. I advise them to do what I have always done: Try for more than you think you can get."

In 1988, for instance, Corey gave a first-year graduate student a problem on which to cut his teeth as a researcher—the synthesis of fluoxetine. Although a pharmaceuticals company had only recently introduced the antidepressant and antiobesity agent, annual sales already totaled $100 million. But synthesizing the drug was tricky, even for the company's experienced chemists. For a green student, it was a tough task. Nevertheless, the student finished his assignment in just six weeks. And he synthesized the drug using a process that was simpler, faster, and more effective than the methods the pharmaceutical company had developed. Corey notes, "I like to give beginning students

*Corey visited the Academy of Sciences and was shown a display by Secretary Solgerg Bjorn-Rasmussen.*

something to build up their confidence."

The key to the student's stunning success was another invention of Corey's: chemzymes. He coined the word by combining "chemical" with "enzymes." Enzymes are proteins that function as biological catalysts, speeding up chemical reactions and making them more efficient, without being consumed in the process. In chemzymes, Corey has produced artificial enzymes, which chemists can use in the synthesis of a range of molecules, gaining greater control over the reactions than they ever had before. *Science*, the journal of the American Association for the Advancement of Science, has said chemzymes

"are fast gaining a reputation among chemists generally as being among the most intriguing innovations of the decade."

Chemzymes act like submicroscopic assembly-line robots. In fact, Corey has dubbed them "molecular robots." Out of the surrounding solution, the chemzyme grabs just the right molecules, fastens them together into the correct three-dimensional assemblage, and then tosses the assemblage into the "finished" bin to get ready to assemble a new set of molecules.

As an added talent, chemzymes can produce molecules of only one orientation, or "chirality." Molecules can be produced as mirror images, with a left one and a right one, like shoes and gloves. What is especially valuable about chemzymes for an organic chemist is that they make the target molecule in only one chirality. If they were making shoes, they would make only left or only right shoes. That is important because an organic molecule will fit into cell receptors only if it has the correct chirality. A receptor shaped to receive a left molecule will reject a right molecule. As a result, a drug with the wrong chirality will prove ineffective.

Ordinary methods of synthesizing compounds produce both left-handed and right-handed versions, willy-nilly. For a pharmaceutical company, that is an expensive waste, since approximately half of the product is useless. Natural enzymes, which might solve the problem, are poorly understood and difficult to harness. As a result, Corey's invention of chemzymes should stimulate the production of medicines and other chemicals.

When he was selected to receive the 1990 chemistry prize, Corey said that he did not see his work as something confined to a laboratory. Rather, he said, it is "a way to improve the health of all people and to make the world a better place for all mankind." The Royal Swedish Academy of Sciences honored Corey's work for having "contributed to the high standards of living and health, and the longevity, enjoyed at least in the Western world."

Corey says he has never distinguished between teaching and research. He and his wife, Claire, have two sons and a daughter, but he regards the hundreds of

---

## THE FAMILY
### (Interview)

There are three children. The eldest is our son David who is now twenty-seven. He got his Ph.D. in bio-organic chemistry at Berkeley and is now doing a post-op. That's very exciting for us. Our second son is John, twenty-five, and he is studying music in Paris. He is at the Paris Conservatory and has just gotten his diploma and is doing some advance work. He wants to be a composer. Our third child is our daughter, Susan, who has just graduated from Harvard with a degree in anthropology. She is interested in Central America, and she wants to do some work—probably in education and teaching, so she is going to be a graduate student.

"I think E. J.'s main love outside of his work is music. John was exposed very early to music all the time, so I think that may have been the beginnings of his interest.

"When John was a student at Harvard he would come home frequently to use the piano, so I could hear music all day. He is very interested in early recordings of music, of classical singers. He has a collection of those sorts of recordings, and I can hear those.

"E. J. never had the chance to have lessons, but he can play by ear a little, and he likes to do that. The children play, which is wonderful. When John is here on vacation, it's just marvelous because he practices quite a number of hours every day—the piano, the viola, the violin. Sometimes some of his friends come and play chamber music, and it is just nonstop pleasure to have him around."—Claire Corey

*Corey and his wife, Claire, frame a portrait of Emanuel Swedenborg. Mrs. Corey has an undergraduate degree in chemistry.*

students who have passed through his laboratory as an extended family. "My research family has been an extraordinarily important part of my life," he says. Teaching has been a key tenet of his personal credo: "To be creative over a broad range of the chemical sciences, to sustain that creativity over many years, to raise the power of research in chemistry to a qualitatively higher level, and to develop new generations of outstanding chemists."

Another chemistry laureate, Dudley Herschbach, who is a longtime friend and Harvard associate of Corey's, compares the syntheses produced in Corey's laboratory to great music: "Like Beethoven and Mahler, he takes the equivalent of simple notes and rhythms and puts them together into marvelous creative works." And just as Corey has mastered the science of reducing complicated molecules to their simplest components, Herschbach sums up Elias Corey's career in a simple sentence: "E. J. has changed the whole way that modern chemistry is done." ∎

*Nobel Prize laureates Donnall Thomas and Joseph Murray discuss a question at a press conference in Stockholm's Grand Hotel.*

# CHAPTER 4

# THE NOBEL PRIZE IN PHYSIOLOGY OR MEDICINE

## THE WORK OF PROFESSOR JOSEPH E. MURRAY, AND PROFESSOR E. DONNALL THOMAS

*The professors were cited "for their discoveries concerning organ and cell transplantation in the treatment of human disease." Joseph Murray developed a surgical technique for kidney transplantation, and today about 20,000 kidneys are transplanted every year. Donnall Thomas managed to diminish the graft-versus-host reaction with drugs and showed that it was possible to cure leukemia and certain other disorders. Bone marrow transplantation has given normal life to more than 10,000 patients.*
*—Professor Gosta Gahrton, member*
*of the Nobel Assembly at the*
*Karolinska Institute*

Traditionally, Nobel laureates in physiology or medicine have been men or women engaged in basic medical science. Well known to a small circle of peers with whom they have exchanged ideas or research results over the years, they are only rarely familiar to the public, the very people whose lives their work may so deeply affect. This year's two prizewinners are pleasing exceptions. Not quite the family doctors of fond memory, they are the sort of "in up to their necks" clinicians after whom grateful patients name children, while their parallel contributions to the advance of medicine were conceived and carried out not in the reflective isolation of the lab but in the dramatic theater of the operating room and the cancer ward.

Dr. Joseph E. Murray of Milford, Massachusetts, successfully performed the first transplant of a human organ in 1954, and Dr. E. Donnall Thomas, of Seattle, Washington, first transplanted bone marrow

*Murray pioneered organ transplants.*

from a human donor to a recipient in 1956. In awarding them the 1990 Nobel Prize in physiology or medicine, the Nobel Committee acknowledged several aspects of a changed medical environment. Among these are the increasing significance of clinically driven science, the emergence of the hybrid physician-researcher, and the philosophical shift in treatment of disease that human transplantation represents. The committee has, by extension, saluted several generations of team players without whose contributions neither man, however persevering, could have made such a

deep imprint.

Until only a few years before Joseph Murray's successful transfer of a kidney from one identical twin to the other, the ancient ambition of saving lives by means of what Murray and others have termed "spare-parts surgery" was still widely judged to be impossible by many in the medical and scientific communities. Experimental transplants in both animals and humans had been attempted as early as the eighteenth century, but although a degree of progress in surgical methods was made, the actual results proved consistently disappointing. There existed between individuals, concluded Alexis Carrel, the 1912 Nobel laureate, a mysterious "biological force" that would forever pose an insuperable barrier to transplants. As late as the end of the 1940s, this notion of an antagonistic and insurmountable "biological force" was still being cited as a probably permanent obstacle to human organ transplantation by no less a figure than immunologist and 1960 Nobel laureate Sir Peter Medawar.

Within a few years, however, the work of both Carrel and Medawar would help demonstrate that their pessimism had been misplaced. Medawar's work on immunological tolerance would provide part of the theoretical underpinning for transplants between unrelated individuals; Carrel's innovative methods of vascular suturing would make possible the last imaginative leap in surgical technique necessary for successful organ transplantation.

In 1943 and 1946, however, as Joseph

*Murray's family gathered around after the Nobel Prize ceremony in Concert Hall.*

Murray and Donnall Thomas, respectively, were finishing up at Harvard Medical School, the possibility of any kind of human transplantation appeared remote. Assigned to a U.S. Army plastic surgery unit in late 1944, after a year's training at Peter Bent Brigham Hospital in Boston (now the Brigham and Women's Hospital), Murray got a firsthand look at the difficulties involved in tissue transplantation. For three years he performed skin grafts on badly burned GIs, many of whom had an insufficient amount of healthy skin of their own to be grafted onto damaged areas. In the worst cases, Murray would later recall, "allografts from family or cadavers were required as temporary skin dressings," but all such allografts were by definition short-lived, being "rejected, with a vigor proportional to the degree of the genetic disparity" between donor and recipient as the phenomenon is described in the fifth edition of *Principles of Surgery*.

The only grafts known to take permanently were those between identical twins, about which Murray heard in more detail from the unit's plastic surgical chief, James Barrett Brown of St. Louis, who had reported on successful reciprocal skin grafts between monozygotic twins a decade earlier. Murray was of course

*Thomas diminished graft-versus-host reaction.*

intrigued by the specifically plastic aspects, but his interest was more broadly engaged as well. If skin grafts between twins were possible, Murray speculated, why not organ transplants as well? It did not seem too great a leap, and "while scrubbing or operating," he later recalled, "we often talked about tissue transplantation, especially about the optimism of surgeons and the pessimism of basic scientists."

On returning to Boston in 1947, Murray joined the experimental transplant group

at Peter Bent Brigham organized by Dr. Francis D. Moore, chief of surgery, and Dr. George W. Thorn, chief of medicine. The team was headed by surgeon Dr. David M. Hume, with whom Murray had been a surgical interne three years earlier, and nephrologist Dr. John P. Merrill. At the time, patients with end-stage renal disease could be kept alive only temporarily with the help of an "artificial kidney," a dialysis machine devised by Dr. Willem Kollf and improved by Dr. Carl Walter at Brigham.

The available surgical treatment was a renal allograft—an exterior hookup of a donor kidney that was surgically attached to the patient's thigh with the urine collected in a bag. While this procedure, pioneered by Hume, did not avert the problem of tissue rejection inherent in a transplant from another individual, it was successful longer than experimental animal transplants had been, and it therefore gave physicians the opportunity to study and monitor the progress of this third kidney.

Although the temporary function improved the patient's condition in some instances for several weeks, the procedure remained far from satisfactory—especially from the patient's point of view. Murray and Hume thus began their surgical work together, trying to devise "better ways to provide adequate skin coverage to the thigh kidney," but their ultimate goal had now become clear.

Hume had already completed a small number of kidney transplants in dogs, but at that time his major experimental interest was the study of the hypothalamic-pitu-

*At a reception at the Karolinska Institute, Thomas and his family posed for photographers.*

itary axis, so he suggested that Murray take over the experimental part of the renal transplant program. Continuing to experiment, Murray by 1954 had successfully transplanted single kidneys into a number of dogs and had worked out the surgical procedures that remain the prototype for renal transplantation in humans today. By the time identical twins, one in terminal uremia and the other healthy, were referred to the Brigham for treatment in 1954, Murray recalled in a recent issue of the *Chimera,* no one was readier than the handsomely supported team at the Brigham.

"We had on hand expertise in renal disease, dialysis and a proven laboratory model for the surgical transplant operation," Murray wrote. Two days before Christmas, using "the exact technique developed in the dog," the thirty-five-year-old surgeon performed the transplant. It was an exhilarating marriage of long preparation and calculated daring, and it proved immediately successful. "Kidney transplants seem so routine now," Murray observed in an interview following the announcement of his award, "but the first one was like Lindbergh's flight across the ocean."

The Brigham's great success predictably ignited worldwide interest in the possibilities of transplantation. Only one year before, the immunological team of Billingham, Brent, and Medawar had issued a report demonstrating that the longstanding "immunological barrier" to transplantation between genetically diverse mice could in fact be surmounted. With Murray having resolved the basic surgical issues, transplants between nonidentical donors were now plausible. It was only a matter of time.

Like researchers and clinicians in scores of universities and teaching hospitals around the world, the Brigham team now turned its attention to the many practical problems involved in nonidentical transplants. These included the procurement and care of donor organs and, most significantly, the circumvention of a reaction of the host against the graft by some form of immune suppression. Initially this was accomplished by X-irradiation, later by the use of antimetabolite drugs, 6-mercaptopurine and its derivative, azathioprine.

Although it had been assumed that the opportunity to transplant a kidney from a healthy identical twin to one in end-stage renal disease would be a once-in-a-lifetime occurrence, within the space of a few years "we were surprised to have to treat several more sets of monozygotic twins," among them a set of identical twin sisters transplanted in 1956. When the sister who received the transplanted kidney gave birth to her first child at Brigham and Women's two years later, Joe Murray was in eager attendance. That patient is now a grandmother and the longest-surviving transplant recipient in the world.

Over the next several years, Murray and his transplant group continued to experiment with new and better drugs to suppress the immune system. In 1959, they performed a successful renal transplant from a non-identical twin using total body X-ray treatment for immunosuppression. However, this was the only success in twelve attempts, so the search for more predictable methods continued. By 1962, using drugs initially pioneered by Schwartz in rabbits, and Calne and Zukoski in dogs, they had begun transplanting kidneys taken from both relatives and cadavers. Despite long preparation, cross-genetic transplants represented a dramatic departure from the comparatively uncomplicated successes of the previous decade, and initial expectations were low. "We all believed it would work," recalled Dr. Charles Carpenter, who had joined the team that year, "but we were afraid it would work in just 20 percent or less and be viewed as a tragic experiment." In fact, about half of that first group of patients survived, including one who is still living. Since 1962, more than 95,000 kidney transplants have been performed in the United States, with a ten-year survival rate of more than 70 percent.

The equally significant result of the Brigham breakthrough was the string of successful transplant "firsts" that followed in short order: first pancreas, in 1966 in Minnesota; first liver, in 1967 in Colorado; first heart, in 1968 in California; first lung transplants, in Toronto, 1980; first heart and lung, 1981. Though problems of toxicity while achieving immunosuppression remain and pose a formidable obstacle for

*Princess Lilian and Murray shared conversation at the Nobel banquet.*

many patients, "the state of the art," according to Dr. Robert Corry, a past president of the National Organ Procurement Transplantation Program, "is currently limited only by donor shortage."

Dr. Murray, who was born in 1919, likes challenge in his personal life too. On his fiftieth birthday he climbed the Matterhorn, and he and his wife have hiked several times in the Himalayas. In his "retirement," he serves as an administrator at Harvard Medical School.

Though in many respects a parallel journey, the path to "state of the art" bone marrow transplantation proved longer, bumpier, and, to the extent that success

was delayed, more controversial. Fourteen years elapsed between the initial successful transfer of marrow from one identical twin to the other performed by E. Donnall Thomas in 1956 and a successful transplant of marrow from a nonidentical sibling. Along the way, as Thomas recently observed, "most people left the field. They felt this couldn't ever be done."

Thomas explains, "Marrow transplantation is inherently much more difficult than solid organ transplants. In marrow grafting we had to take major detours in radiation biology, transplantation biology, immunology, infectious diseases including virology, cytogenetics, immunogenetics,

61

cancer biology and chemotherapy and transfusion medicine—just to mention some disciplines."

An instructor in medicine at Harvard Medical School and a hematologist on the staff of Peter Bent Brigham at the time of Joseph Murray's first kidney transplant in 1954, Thomas had long explored the same territory as a potential treatment for leukemia, an invariably fatal disease at the time and one that in several of its forms continues to resist even the most dramatic recent advances in curative chemotherapy.

Starting in the early 1950s, Thomas conducted experiments with dogs. First, the animal's own marrow was destroyed with radiation and cytotoxic drugs, and then, healthy donor marrow was introduced into its veins by intravenous drip. In theory, the donor marrow would migrate to the center of the animal's bones, where it would take hold and begin producing new marrow—technically a much simpler process than organ transplantation. When Thomas carried out the first such transfer of marrow, between identical twins in 1956, the process worked just as he had hoped. Subsequent attempts to transplant marrow between unrelated individuals, however, proved immunologically disastrous.

Patients were caught in immunological pincers: Either the patient's original immune system would attack the donor, or "foreign," marrow as it recovered from its artificially induced suppression, or the donor marrow, itself composed of immune system cells, would read the patient's healthy organs as hostile and launch an all-out, ultimately fatal assault of its own.

The period between 1956 and 1970 was, according to one transplantation pioneer, "hellish." Patients, most of them young, died of drug toxicity, infection, or graft-versus-host disease. If there were to be any hope of making marrow transplantation a worthwhile therapy, improvements would have to be made at every stage of the process, from increasing the degree of histocompatibility between donor and recipient, to improving the quality of immune suppression before and following transplantation, to ensuring protection against infection for these uniquely vulnerable patients.

In order to be saved, patients had to endure a months-long ordeal in which they were artificially brought to the brink, and then suspended in an austere and isolated medical limbo while they waited to discover whether the new marrow would take hold. With a short-term survival rate hovering around 10 percent, it was a gamble ill-suited to the fainthearted, and only a handful of physicians persisted. "Some people thought it was a very dangerous and unwarranted thing to do to patients," recalled Dr. Patrick Beatty, head of the University of Utah's bone marrow transplant unit, and only very few pressed on.

Donnall Thomas was foremost among them. Working in close collaboration with his wife, Dorothy, he assiduously incorporated each successive refinement in immunological testing, cytotoxic drugs, and increasingly sophisticated techniques in

*Thomas escorted Mrs. Charles E. Redman, wife of the U.S. ambassador to Sweden, into the banquet hall.*

posttransplant patient care in order to optimize the chance of a cure for patients with no other option.

In June 1970, while heading the oncology division at the University of Washington School of Medicine in Seattle, Thomas finally succeeded. The patient was a sixteen-year-old girl dying of leukemia whose brother donated his marrow. It was the first instance of a closely, but not perfectly, HLA-matched marrow transplant surviving in host and, as such, the precursor of a flood of such procedures. Though bone marrow transplants would continue to be considered experimental—essentially a treatment of last resort—for another full

decade, Thomas had demonstrated that the seemingly insuperable obstacles to transfer of this most sensitive immunological tissue could be overcome.

During the last ten years, following the pattern established in organ transplantation, bone marrow transfers have become, if not quite routine, very much standard treatment for several forms of leukemia and for a number of rare blood diseases and disorders, such as immunodeficiency, aplastic anemia, and thalassemia. Prior to 1968, no more than 203 marrow transplants had been reported in the scientific literature, none of them successful. From 1970 through 1978, the annual number of

**I**n Cooperstown I did a lot of the animal and patient work. I did all the hematology on the early patients, and when we came here [Seattle] I did a fair amount in the lab, although I wasn't working full time. Our daughter was younger then, and Don was just getting started with not much grant support, not much funding. He couldn't pay technicians for weekend work. So for about two or three years I did the hematology on the weekends and covered. I was a volunteer then.

"There weren't any breakthroughs. It's just a long and tedious process of working slowly at something, just hacking away at it, peeling it off like layers. We've just done that. You have to depend on input from a lot of other people too. For instance, histo-compatibility typing came along, and that made it much easier to find suitable matches. It's long, slow work by a lot of people.

"I don't think my presence has been an inspiration. I think it's been a help simply because— particularly in the last fifteen years as I got more and more into the administrative end of things— I've run the office. I've tried to free Don from doing a lot of things that he might otherwise have had to do. I've done a lot of manuscript editing and worked hard on grant preparation.

"I screen Don from people. I'm known as the Dragon Lady. You can't get in unless you get past me, but I don't think that's particularly inspiring. It's just something that has to be done.

"Five or six years ago someone asked me to write a job description of what I did. I thought for a long while, and I finally wrote: 'I cope.'"— Dorothy Thomas

transplants climbed from an average of 80 to 200, the number of new transplant teams from five to twelve. Today close to 3,000 bone marrow transplants are performed annually by teams at nearly three hundred institutions in more than forty countries. In the United States alone, marrow transplant teams are available in sixty cities in thirty states, the largest of them being Thomas's Fred Hutchison Cancer Center in Seattle, where 350 transplants are performed each year. One of his former pupils summed up his mentor's contributions by saying, "Virtually every major transplant center in the world got its start by sending someone to train under Don Thomas."

Thomas says that during his time in Cooperstown, Dr. Joseph Ferrebee was a major collaborator. "My principal colleagues in Seattle," Thomas says, "have been Dr. Dean Buckner, Alex Fefer, Paula Neiman, and Rainer Storb. These individuals have been in the program since the mid-1960s. All are full professors, and all have won major prizes in their own right."

In explaining the importance of Thomas's contributions, *The Scientist* calls him a "superstar." His most cited article is the first installment of a two-part series that reviews research on bone marrow transplants in rodents, dogs, primates, and human patients . . . this state-of-the-art review article has received close to 12,800 citations.

Thomas was born in Mart, Texas, in 1920. He and his wife have three children, two of whom are doctors. Throughout his career, his wife has helped with the man-

*Among those on stage at the Nobel presentation ceremony were, from left: Elias Corey, Joseph Murray, Donnall Thomas, and Octavio Paz.*

agement of his research and with his papers. Dr. George Santos of Johns Hopkins says that if Dr. Thomas is the father of bone marrow transplants, "then Dottie Thomas is the mother."

As for Joseph Murray, who returned to plastic surgery late in his distinguished career and devoted himself to correcting congenital facial deformities in children, his longtime superior, Francis Moore, when asked to comment on his friend's receipt of the Nobel, hesitated not a moment before framing his admiration as bluntly as he could: "Well, I nominated him for it." ■

*The Nobel Prize laureate Dr. Octavio Paz.*

# CHAPTER 5

# THE NOBEL PRIZE IN LITERATURE

## THE WORK OF DR. OCTAVIO PAZ

*The prize citation—"for impassioned writing with wide horizons, charac-*
*terized by sensuous intelligence and humanistic integrity"—indicates*
*what is perhaps most immediately striking in his writing:*
*his passion and his integrity.*
*—Professor Kjell Espmark, Member of the*
*Swedish Academy, Chairman of its*
*Nobel Committee for Literature*

*Between what I see and what I say*
*Between what I say and what I*
    *keep silent*
*Between what I keep silent and*
    *what I dream*
*Between what I dream and what I*
    *forget:*
*Poetry.*

Octavio Paz—poet, essayist, diplomat, libertarian in verse and in
life—is a worldly man and a man
of the world. He is at home among his
literary peers in the universities as well as
in the chancelleries of power on several
continents. His roots are in Mexico, in
ancient Indian legends and lore, yet he is
equally comfortable in the international
company of democratic idealists who
continue to believe in Rousseau's social

contract: There remains a need for a country's rulers to safeguard the rights and
improve the lot of all its citizens. These
classical ideas are deeply embedded in his
writings. No matter what emerges from his
pen—surrealism, eroticism, hemispheric
dreams, experimental forms—Paz is fundamentally a sophisticated man of letters.

What distinguishes his work is that he
succeeds in linking his personal mytholo-
gy with world concerns, which are made
to flow out of, and then into, his own life.
One of his first major books of poetry,
*Sunstone*, focuses on the Aztec calendar
stone but then moves into the modern
reality of Mexico. The ancient calendar is
based on the conjunctions of Venus and
the sun; Paz matches the 584 days of this
cycle with 584 lines of poetry. Some of its
lines, employing elemental language, il-

lustrate his preoccupation with the sensual and romantic nature of mankind:

> *I travel your body, like the world,*
> *Your belly is a plaza full of sun,*
> *Your breasts two churches where*
>     *blood*
> *Performs its own parallel rites.*

In recent years, Paz has shown his ability to keep up with the times, including the new emphasis on women's rights. He believes that there is a fundamental distinction between men and women and that femininity should be cherished.

Yet the subject he chose for a biographical portrait, *Sor Juana: or The Traps of Faith,* is a remarkable seventeenth-century woman, Juana Inés de la Cruz, a Mexican poet and dramatist who later became a nun. Paz placed her life against the background of the society of her own time. Modern readers admire the book's lessons—and the fact that Paz reached back into the past to depict a woman who succeeded in breaking out of the strictures of her culture. Paz's great admiration of her literary versatility is considered an example of his own generosity of spirit. He rages at the repression that forced her to renounce her gifts and beliefs as a writer in favor of a show of orthodox piety.

Whether using Spanish, French, or English, Paz employs a polished prose characterized by the balanced phrasing of a diplomat. In this respect, his spoken language and written language are similar. When writing in Spanish, he uses a classi-cal meter without rhymes. "Blank verse," he says, "like Wordsworth or Milton. But I use rhythm in my poetry and calculate everything."

The influences on his writing have shifted slowly over the years. Once he was interested in the Romantic poets, especially Shelley and Keats, though the mystical William Blake was his first great love. Later the Americans Whitman and Thoreau attracted him. His discovery of the moderns, especially T. S. Eliot, caused him to turn back to John Donne and the seventeenth-century poets. From the French, including Baudelaire, he learned about surrealism. Then, under the influence of pre-Columbian culture and the Buddhist philosophy of India and Japan, he evolved his own style of free verse, one rooted in the classics of various countries but at the service of modern themes.

In personal appearance, Paz is of medium height, with a crown of graying black hair above a gentle face and stocky frame. In their elegance, his manners match his casual, professorial attire. He listens and puts a visitor at ease, as if to say, "Never mind, everything will be all right." And then, with a smile, he adds only half-ironically, "Well, eventually."

Of his new laurels, Paz says, "The Nobel Prize is not a passport to immortality. But it does give a poet the possibility of a wider audience—and all writers need to broaden their readership. The Nobel is a kind of challenge. I hope to continue to be self-critical. I've been around too long—after all, I was born in 1914—to either stop writing or to be the sole judge of my own

*P*rofessor Sture Allén, permanent secretary of the Swedish Academy, greeted Paz and his wife, Marie José, at the airport.

work. To me, a poet represents not only a region but the universe. Language is the common property of society, and all writers should be the guardians of language. A writer has two loyalties. First, he belongs to the special tribe of writers. Second, he belongs to a culture, to his own country. In my case, it is Mexico."

Paz is very conscious, without being self-conscious, of his personal duality as a poet and diplomat, of being an individual and a member of a larger community of artists and statesmen.

"We are all born alone and writers must write alone," he says. "Still, there is a need for human communication. A poet has to write well; he may also be a critic of society. But I am only one voice among many voices. I am aware that I am a descendant of other writers. Beginning when I was very young and continuing later in my life, I have read foreign poetry—Eliot, Breton, Montale, Ungaretti, Calvino, the French surrealists. Poetry crosses borders and barriers. Surrealism may be regarded as dead, but surrealism lives in different forms in different parts of the world."

71

*Princess Christina was escorted down the grand staircase by Octavio Paz.*

*Mixcoac was my village: three
    nocturnal syllables,
a half-mask of shadow across a
    face of sun.
Our Lady, Mother Dustcloud, came,
came and ate it. I went out in the
    world.
My words were my house, air my
    tomb.*

"Yes, sometimes poets do mix in politics—and not always with the greatest intelligence," Paz says, his diplomatic eyebrows raised diplomatically and laugh lines playing around the corners of his mouth. "But we should not forget that the greatest

poet of all, Dante, included a great deal of politics in his poetry. Many writers have been diplomats—for example, Pablo Neruda and St. John Perse. I believe in the need to be an *homme engagé* at certain times. This has been a very cruel century.

"I speak for the generation of the 1930s, which has simultaneously suffered from fascism, Marxism, and revolution. Think of the Nazis, with their concentration camps where millions of Jews and other innocent people were put to death systematically. Think of the poets who died in Stalinist prisons and the oppression visited upon so many men, women, and children by Latin American dictators. Now we are seeing a return to freedom in many corners of the world and the possibility of peaceful solutions to military conflicts. That should be the goal of governments today."

As for his own political inclinations, Paz has sometimes been described as a writer of the Left. He once listed his politics as those of a "disillusioned Leftist." But he says, "I don't write simply on the Left. I very much believe in democracy and the rights of minorities and the underprivileged. Of course, I do have a specific point of view that emerges in my essays. Historically, the Left was born in the eighteenth century, and it came into existence because it was needed. The traditional Left has always been for freedom. But 'Right' and 'Left' are not very useful terms. What we need today are not labels but democracy and peace instead of revolution and war."

*My grandfather, taking his coffee,*
*would talk to me about Juárez and*
     *Porfirio,*
*the Zouaves and the Silver Band.*
*And the tablecloth smelled of*
     *gunpowder.*

*My father, taking his drink,*
*would talk to me about Zapata and*
     *Villa,*
*Soto y Gama and the brothers of Flores*
     *Magon.*
*And the tablecloth smelled of gunpow-*
     *der.*
*I kept quiet:*
*who was there for me to talk about?*

---

## PAZ ON POETS
### (Interview)

**O**ne day when I was a child, I found myself—without knowing—writing a rather childish poem. That was the beginning. I think the old proverb that poets are born is true. But to be born a poet is not enough. Everybody in some way—all mankind, women and men—is born a poet, but only a few persevere. I was one of the few that tried to conquer language—or rather to be conquered by language.

"It is a battle that starts when you are a child, and it goes on all your life. You will never be satisfied with the things you have written, and there is never a final version of a poem. I should say the same perhaps for a novel. Works of art are always unfinished.

"Another thing I believe very strongly is that poets and writers as a rule do only half the job. The other part is done by readers. The reader is another creator of the poem or the short story or the novel because he gives an interpretation.

"A poet is never the owner of his poem. The real owner of a poem is the reader."

Later in life's journey, he had much to talk about. Paz was born in Mexico City, where he still makes his home, on March 13, 1914. The family was of mainly Spanish, but also partly Indian, descent. His paternal grandfather was a public official with liberal ideas and a novelist who was among the first to write sympathetically about Mexico's Indian population, an attitude frequently reflected in the poet's own work. His early contact with literature took place in his grandfather's extensive library.

Paz's father was a lawyer and politician who believed in social reform; he was a pioneer of agrarian reform who joined Emiliano Zapata during the 1910 revolution and represented him in the United States. Paz followed in his father's footsteps by studying law, but he did not take a degree. During the Spanish Civil War, he attended an antifascist congress in Madrid, witnessing the war in sympathy with the Republicans against Franco's insurgents. Afterward, he aided Spanish Republican refugees in Mexico. Paz became one of the editors of the journal *Workshop,* which exerted a strong influence on contemporary literature in his own country.

During World War II, Paz studied in the United States under a Guggenheim fellowship and then entered his country's diplomatic service. He became a diplomat in, successively, France, Switzerland, Japan, and India. In 1968, he resigned as ambassador to India in protest against Mexico's suppression of student demonstrations during the Olympic Games in Mexico. In 1976, he founded and edited *Return,* a journal of literature and political commentary. He was given the 1982 Cervantes Prize, the most important award in the Spanish-speaking world.

*Hear the throbbing of space*
*it is the steps of a season in heat*
*across the embers of the year.*
*Murmur of wings and rattles*
*the far-off drumbeats of the storm*
*the crackling and panting of the*
  *earth*
*under its cape of roots and bugs.*

Paz's ideas continue to be expressed in his books of essays as well as in his verse. His essays combine literature, philosophy, and a strong political interest rooted in history. He has written some thirty books of poetry and prose that have been translated into many languages. Among his major works (with the years they were translated into English) are *The Labyrinth of Solitude: Life and Thought in Mexico* (1961), *Sunstone* (1962), *The Bow and the Lyre* (1973), *Alternating Current* (1973), *Conjunctions and Disjunctions* (1974), *Selected Poems* (1979), *One Earth, Four or Five Days: Reflections on Contemporary History* (1985), *The Collected Poems of Octavio Paz, 1957-1987* (1987), and *Sor Juana: or, The Traps of Faith* (1988).

In 1989, when the shackles of totalitarian regimes began to loosen and the cold war drew to a close, Paz delivered one of his most important statements when he was awarded the Tocqueville Prize in Paris: "Joyce said that history is a nightmare, but nightmares vanish with the light of day, while history will not be over until

*The poet faced the reporters and photographers at a Stockholm press conference.*

our species ends. We are human through history and in it; if it ceased to exist, we would cease to be human. But the end of the revolutionary myth will perhaps permit us to think again about the principles that have founded our society, about their deficiencies and lacunae. Relieved at last of the struggle against totalitarian superstition, we can now reflect more freely on our tradition. And so the theme of the virtue of citizens makes its reappearance.

"It is a theme that comes from classical antiquity; it concerned Machiavelli as well as Montesquieu, and today it has a painful actuality in many countries, including the Anglo-American democracy founded by the Puritan ethic. Kant taught that morality cannot be based on history, since history flows unceasingly, and we do not know if any law or design rules its capricious passing. We also know that metahistorical constructs—religious or metaphysical, conservative or revolutionary—strangle liberty and eventually corrupt fraternity. The thought of the era that is beginning will have to find a point of convergence between liberty and fraternity. We must rethink our tradition, renovate it, and search for the reconciliation of the two great political traditions of modernity—liberalism and socialism."

And then, Paz wondered, what can be the contribution of poetry to the remaking of a new political order? The poet in Paz responded to his own rhetorical question

*A display of Ocatvio Paz's books was set up in the library.*

in shimmering prose: "Not new ideas, but something more precious and fragile: memory. In each generation, the poets rediscover the terrible antiquity, and the no less terrible youth, of passions. In the schools and universities, where the so-called political sciences are taught, the reading of Aeschylus and Shakespeare should be obligatory. Poets nourished the thought of Hobbes and Locke, Marx and Tocqueville. Through the mouth of the poet there speaks—I emphasize speaks, not writes—the other voice, the voice of the tragic poet and the buffoon, the voice of solitary melancholy and of joy, of laughter and of sighs, the voice of the lovers' embrace and of Hamlet contemplating the skull, the voice of silence and of tumult, mad wisdom and wise madness, the intimate murmur in the bedroom and the surging crowd in the square. To hear that voice is to hear time itself, the time that passes and comes back still, transformed into a few crystalline syllables."

> *Shadows of white day*
> *against my eyes. I see*
> *nothing but white:*
> *white hour, soul unchained*
> *from desire, from the hour.*
>
> *Whiteness of still waters,*
> *white hour, blindness of open eyes.*
> *Strike your flint, burn, memory,*
> *against the hour and its undertow.*
> *Memory, swimming flame.* ∎

# FROM OCTAVIO PAZ'S NOBEL LECTURE
(Excerpts)

**P**oetry is in love with the instant and seeks to relive it in the poem, thus separating it from sequential time and turning it into a fixed present. But at that time I wrote without wondering why I was doing it. I was searching for the gateway to the present: I wanted to belong to my time and to my century. . . .

"Each poetic adventure is distinct and each poet has sown a different plant in the miraculous forest of speaking trees . . . the poet is a pulse in the rhythmic flow of generations.

"I need hardly mention what everybody knows: Natural resources are finite and will run out one day. In addition, we have inflicted what may be irreparable damage on the natural environment, and our own species is endangered. Finally, science and technology, the instruments of progress, have shown with alarming clarity that they can easily become destructive forces. The existence of nuclear weapons is a refutation of the idea that progress is inherent in history. This refutation, I add, can only be called devastating. . . .

"Seldom have nations or individuals suffered so much: two world wars, tyrannies spread over five continents, the atomic bomb and the proliferation of one of the cruellest and most lethal institutions known by man—the concentration camp. Modern technology has provided countless benefits, but it is impossible to

*Paz delivers his lecture.*

close our eyes when confronted by slaughter, torture, humiliation, degradation, and other wrongs inflicted on millions of innocent people in our century. . . .

"For the first time in history mankind lives in a sort of spiritual wilderness and not, as before, in the shadow of those religious and political systems that consoled us at the same time as they oppressed us. . . .

"The triumph of the market economy (a triumph due to the adversary's default) cannot be simply a cause for joy. As a mechanism the market is efficient, but like all mechanisms it lacks both conscience and compassion. We must find a way of integrating it into society so that it expresses the social contract and becomes an instrument of justice and fairness. The advanced democratic societies have reached an enviable level of prosperity; at the same time they are islands of abundance in the ocean of universal misery. The topic of the market is intricately related to the deterioration of the environment. Pollution affects not only the air, the rivers, and the forests but also our souls. A society possessed by the frantic need to produce more in order to consume more tends to reduce ideas, feelings, art, love, friendship, and people themselves to consumer products. Everything becomes a thing to be bought, used, and then thrown on the rubbish dump. No other society has produced so much waste as ours has. Material and moral waste."—Translated by Anthony Stanton

*Wherever he goes, President Mikhail Gorbachev, his political grin flashing, works the crowd.*

# CHAPTER 6

# THE NOBEL PRIZE IN PEACE

## THE WORK OF THE PRESIDENT OF THE SOVIET UNION
## MIKHAIL SERGEYEVICH GORBACHEV

*This year's Nobel Peace Prize has been awarded to President Gorbachev in recognition of the leading role he has played in the radical changes that have taken place in East-West relations.*
—*Gidske Anderson, Chairperson of the Norwegian Nobel Committee*

When President Mikhail Gorbachev could not attend the Nobel Prize ceremony in December because pressing domestic problems demanded his presence in Moscow, an Oslo paper ran a cartoon showing him balancing precariously on the edge of the Nobel peace medal while Soviet people were crying out, "But a *bread* prize, Mikhail?"

In fact, when the news of Gorbachev's prize was announced in October, correspondents in Moscow reported that the people were far more interested in where they could find meat, butter, and sugar. One more instance of acclaim in the West for Gorbachev seemed of little consequence. His approval rating in the Soviet Union was already at a new low.

The new laureate was a prophet without much honor in his own country, where his troubles have continued to mount. Not only was he blamed for the critical food shortages, but Soviet liberals, as well as foreign experts, also faulted him for the slow pace of his economic reforms. Meanwhile, conflict was growing between the ethnic groups with different national aspirations and between the republics and the central government, several of which wanted to break away from the Soviet Union. On the Right, the hard-liners called into question Gorbachev's reformist policies and began to clamor for authoritarian measures to restore order. There were signs that Gorbachev himself was being drawn in this direction, and before the month ended, his longtime friend Foreign Minister Eduard Shevardnadze, an original supporter of his reforms and

Blanche Gamma-Liaison

*In Privolnoye, where he was born, President Gorbachev and his wife, Raisa, visit with his mother, Maria. The village is north of the Caucasus.*

the chief implementer of his foreign policy, resigned in a dramatic speech, warning of the forces pushing Gorbachev toward dictatorship.

In view of the uncertain future of the Soviet Union, there were those who thought that the Norwegian Nobel Committee might have waited to award the prize to Gorbachev, but could it have found anyone who had done more for world peace than the statesman who had brought an end to the cold war?  In presenting the tokens of the award to Anatoly Kovalev, the veteran diplomat who represented Gorbachev at the ceremony, Gidske Anderson, the prominent writer who chaired the committee, declared that the prize was granted "in recognition of the leading role Gorbachev has played in the radical changes that have taken place in East-West relations" and that his personal contributions were "decisive." The new East-West climate had made possible significant arms-control agreements, she said, and had "given the United Nations a new lease on life." Moreover, he was responsible for the liberation of the former Soviet satellites in Eastern Europe.

In Gorbachev's acceptance message, which was read by Kovalev at the ceremony, the Soviet president gave assurance that "the leadership of the USSR is doing, and will continue to do, everything in its power to ensure that future developments in Europe and the world as a whole are based on openness, mutual trust, international law, and universal values."

This *glasnost*, or openness, which Gorbachev had introduced in his own country and now pledged to promote in the world, was the one element of his domestic policy that Anderson singled out for praise in her speech, pointing out that it had provided a basis for the disarmament agreements and the other measures of East-West co-operation.

It was on December l6, 1986, that Gorbachev made a symbolic gesture to show the world that the Soviet Union was embarking upon a new era of openness. On that day, he made a surprising telephone call to Andrei Sakharov, who had been banished to internal exile in Gorki in 1980 for daring to denounce the Soviet invasion of Afghanistan. The scientist, whom the official press had reviled as a traitor in l975 when he had been granted the Nobel Peace Prize for his courageous stand for human rights, was now invited back to Moscow by Gorbachev to continue his "patriotic work."

As Gorbachev encouraged the winds of freedom to blow, other political detainees were released, free criticism of the government was permitted in the press, freer elections were held, and historians were able to write about Soviet history as it actually had happened. Finally, in 1990, Gorbachev moved to eliminate the constitutional monopoly of power of the Communist Party in the Soviet Union.

Sakharov had always maintained that the Soviet Union needed to become a more open society before it could be trusted to keep its international commitments. With his policy of *glasnost,* Gorbachev could now take actions in the international arena that the Nobel Committee considered decisive, not only reversing long-standing Kremlin policy but personally convincing President Ronald Reagan and his successor, George Bush, that such changes were substantive, not cosmetic. His personal role here was crucial.

Only eight months after coming to power in March 1985, Gorbachev had the first of his four summit meetings with Reagan, establishing a personal relationship that led the American president to give up his conception of the Soviet Union as an "evil empire" long before many of his fellow conservatives at home.

A key move in ending the cold war was Gorbachev's withdrawal of troops from Afghanistan after the bitter ten-year war there. More surprising was his decision that Soviet security no longer needed the buffer of Soviet satellites in Eastern Europe, the area from which foreign invaders had traditionally marched against Russia; he stayed the hand of would-be interventionists and allowed Communist governments in the region to collapse and free governments to arise.

By offering disproportionate cuts in Soviet weapons, Gorbachev negotiated an arms agreement with the United States. Finally, and with great hesitation, ever mindful of the tremendous Soviet losses during the German invasion of World War II, he agreed to the reunification of Germany and its membership in NATO.

How did the rigid, closed-minded Soviet system produce such an innovative spirit as Gorbachev? From the beginning, there were certain influences that could have nourished qualities alien to the typ-

*At a reception in the Kremlin, the president shared a toast with Raisa, his wife and confidante.*

ical Soviet bureaucrat. He was the child of peasants in the northern Caucasus whose ancestors had moved there from central Russia and the Ukraine to seek a freer life than serfdom. The family was religious and hid its icons from watchful Communists; Gorbachev's mother even had him baptized, although he never became a believer.

Mikhail "Misha" Sergeyevitch Gorbachev was born in 1931, far from Moscow in the village of Privolnoye, in the province of Stavropol, where his parents lived in a simple two-room hut. It was the time of Stalin's collectivization of the peasants through brutal methods of terror

and induced famine. The Gorbachev family, with their own land and livestock, were classed as "middle peasants"—one level below the *kulaks*, or rich peasants, who were completely liquidated—and, as such, were officially viewed as antisocial and subject to repressive measures.

How difficult it was for his family Gorbachev has revealed only recently. One grandfather, he said, "was denounced for not fulfilling the sowing plan in 1933, a year when half the family died of hunger," and was sent to Siberia. Grandfather Gopkolo, on Gorbachev's Ukrainian side, had moved with the tide, contributed his own land, and taken the lead in organizing

83

collectives, but he, too, fell victim to the organized terror and was in prison for fourteen months. "They interrogated him, demanded that he admit what he'd never done. Thank God, he survived." But when he returned home, he was considered an "enemy of the people," and even relatives could not visit him, "otherwise 'they' would have come after them too."

Misha's father was a combine operator and eventually became leader of a tractor brigade. But it was his mother, who still lives in Privolnoye, who was the stronger one, always speaking at local meetings— often, as a teetotaler, denouncing the drunkards.

An achiever with leadership talents from the start, Misha did well in school. When Germany attacked the Soviet Union in 1941, his father was called to the army. In 1942, German forces occupied the Privolnoye area for some months, and Misha had to leave school and work in the fields with the women and the old men. People who could not read would come to him to hear the newspapers read aloud and to have him explain what was happening in the war.

Misha was encouraged by Grandfather Gopkolo to continue with his studies at the

*After years of strained relations, Gorbachev had a historic meeting with China's Deng Xiaoping.*

nearest high school—fifteen miles away—to which he walked every week, boarding with relatives and friends and taking the long walk home for weekends. When his father returned after the war, Misha was a mature teenager who could work along with him, driving a combine, during summer vacations. In one harvest they made such extraordinary efforts that they were both awarded the Red Banner of Labor, an unusual honor for a seventeen-year-old.

In high school Misha became a leader of the Komsomol, the Communist Youth Organization, and before he graduated, he applied to, and was selected as a "candidate member" of, the Communist Party. This political activity, along with his excellent academic record and his labor medal, helped bring about his admission in 1950 to prestigious Moscow State University, where his political career began in earnest.

As a law student, this farm boy with a provincial education was competing with decorated war veterans and privileged sons and daughters of Moscow officials. That his success story continued is testimony both to his natural gifts and to his resolve and dedication. While the curriculum emphasized authoritative texts of Marxism-Leninism and Stalin's speeches and writings, the law courses honed his mind, and in studying political theory, he read Greek and medieval philosophers, as well as Machiavelli, Hobbes, Montesquieu, and Rousseau.

He was also exposed to Western influences through his close friendship with the Czech student, Zdenek Mlynar, who lived in his dormitory. Mlynar, who was to rise high in the party in his own country but had to emigrate after the suppression of the Prague Spring in 1968, has recalled that Gorbachev was "naturally intelligent, gifted, able to overcome all the limitations and barriers of a peasant boy coming to Moscow for the first time. He possessed a kind of open-mindedness, not merely an adaptability, but an openness." And he had an insatiable desire to learn about everything. Mlynar remembers his asking somebody, "What's ballet? Tell me, what's it about?" His education in higher culture was soon taken in hand by Raisa Titorenko, the bright and attractive philosophy student whom he married while they were still at the university.

Gorbachev soon became the Komsomol organizer for his class and then for the whole law faculty. Fellow students remember him as a strict disciplinarian in this position, never straying from the party line and always seeking to remain in the good graces of higher-level party members. Yet, he had no hesitation in standing up for a Jewish friend who was the target of anti-Semitic insults.

Having been indoctrinated since childhood with admiration for the "great leader" Stalin, Gorbachev, like most of his fellow students, was a dedicated Stalinist, and the death of Stalin in 1953 was a time of great grief. But in 1956, after he had graduated and gone back to Stavropol with Raisa to take a new position in the Komsomol, Gorbachev's feelings for Stalin suffered a sea change. The new leader, Nikita Khrushchev, in his secret speech at the Twentieth Party Congress, revealed the truth about Stalin and his crimes. Up to that time, Gorbachev had shared with close friends his memories of some of his family's cruel experiences during the collectivization, but he had not criticized Stalin. Now his sense of betrayal, not by Soviet Communism, but by its perversion by Stalin, must have welled up strongly within him. Khrushchev's de-Stalinization policies were ended when he was replaced by Leonid Brezhnev in 1964, but many of the young people like Gorbachev who were in their twenties and thirties at the time of Khrushchev's revelations and reforms did not give up their ideals and came to be called "the children of the Twentieth Congress."

In his twenty-three years as a party functionary in Stavropol, Gorbachev was motivated by such ideals to work hard at his jobs, to become a model administrator, and to keep himself free from the corruption with which the party apparatus was riddled. He kept his criticisms to himself, faithfully followed the party line, and skillfully curried favor with highly placed party protectors.

He had unusual opportunities to develop such useful connections when he was promoted at age thirty-nine to the top party position in Stavropol province and hosted vacationing Politburo leaders who came from Moscow to take the waters at the noted spas of the region. After eight years in this position, he was called to Moscow in 1978 to join the party secretariat with responsibility for agriculture. The next year, he was elected candidate member of the Politburo and in 1980 became a

full member. At the age of forty-nine, Gorbachev had risen to membership in the highest governing body of the country.

In 1982, Brezhnev was succeeded as general secretary by Yuri Andropov, Gorbachev's special protector, whose reform efforts were cut short by his death in 1984. The old guard then returned to power with the election of the already ailing Konstantin Chernenko, who died in 1985. With the country facing an economic crisis, the able and energetic Gorbachev was clearly the most qualified candidate for the post of general secretary, but his election by the Party Central Committee was not a sure thing and was only decided by the nominating speech of the respected longtime foreign minister, Andrei Gromyko. "Comrades," Gromyko is reported to have said, "this man has a nice smile but he's got steel teeth."

Gorbachev made it to the top by doing business the old way, as a supreme conformist. Now, as a child of the Twentieth Congress, he was determined to clean up the Augean stables of the privileged and corrupt party bureaucracy and to get his country's economy moving again. As he explained later, "We came to the conclusion that we could no longer continue to live the way we were. We needed major changes in every department of life."

The distinction must be made between his role abroad and at home. In the sphere of international politics, he was freer to take decisive action, unhindered by the kind of political structure that made Western leaders responsible to elective bodies. Prompted by the realization that a

*On a visit to Poland in 1988, Gorbachev attended a friendship meeting between the youths of Poland and the USSR.*

strong Soviet economy demanded an end to the arms race, with the huge military expenditures needed to keep up with the West, Gorbachev was prepared from the beginning to change direction and make concessions, even though he surely was not aware of how far he would have to go in revolutionizing Soviet relationships with the West.

Domestically, it was very different. Gorbachev was limited in his reforms not only by the resistance of the entrenched party bureaucrats to their loss of privilege and by popular inertia but also by his own deeply held ideological convictions. As

Gidske Anderson declared in her speech, "Our laureate has in fact been a Communist all his life; and he still is to this day."

"I've been told more than once that it is time to stop swearing allegiance to socialism," Gorbachev said recently. "Why should I? Socialism is my deep conviction, and I will promote it as long as I can talk and work." What he wants is "a humane, democratic socialism that joins a socialist approach with individual interests."

He would vigorously dispute any suggestion that for seventy years the Soviet Union has been on the wrong track. "Am I supposed to turn my back on my grandfather, who was committed to the [socialist] idea?" he asks. "And I cannot go against my father, who defended Kursk, forded the Dnieper knee-deep in blood and was wounded in Czechoslovakia [in World War II]. When cleansing myself of Stalinism and all other filth, should I renounce my grandfather and father and all they did?"

Gorbachev did not set out with a vision of revolutionizing Soviet society; he simply wanted to reform persisting evils of Stalinism. But each step he took led him to the next step, and eventually he found that the forces he had set in motion were to have far-reaching consequences that he had not intended. First, he had hopes for the new party leadership; then he turned to the party rank and file to energize the top party echelons; and next, with *glasnost,* he gave freedom to the people as a whole to criticize and stir up the party. *Perestroika* was never meant to restructure the political system to remove the party's right to rule. When Sakharov was demanding a multiparty system, Gorbachev argued with him, but a few months later he acted to change the Soviet Constitution to bring it about. With *perestroika* Gorbachev moved away from the centralized command economy but not to a complete market economy.

*Glasnost* opened the floodgates to the powerful nationalist movements that now threaten to tear the Soviet Union apart. It remains to be seen whether Gorbachev can negotiate an acceptable agreement with independent republics that would keep them in a federated Soviet Union or whether he will feel that force must be used to preserve the union.

The struggle goes on in the Soviet Union between the reformers, who want Gorbachev to move further toward decentralized markets and political democracy, and the conservatives, who want centralized control and presidential action to restore order. The drama plays itself out in a country that in its long history has known a form of liberal democracy only for a few months in 1917 after the fall of the czar and before the Bolshevik seizure of power. Pessimistic prognosticators look to a return to authoritarianism, even totalitarianism, either with Gorbachev in power or overturned by the military and the hardliners. Optimists say that Gorbachev takes the middle position between the extremists, that he is, after all, a survivor, and that he will find the way to feed his country, stabilize it, and then continue on the course of *perestroika.*

These are the pressing problems that kept Gorbachev from collecting his prize in Oslo in person. Some observers, and perhaps Gorbachev himself, believe that the Nobel Committee made the grant of the prize to help keep him afloat in his sea of troubles at home. Toward the end of her presentation speech, Gidske Anderson did refer to the award "as a helping hand in an hour of need." But elsewhere she declared, "This is neither the time nor the place to discuss the Soviet Union's *internal* affairs. The Norwegian Nobel Committee has given President Gorbachev the Peace Prize for his leading role in international politics."

## GORBACHEV'S ACCEPTANCE REMARKS
### (Excerpt)

In his time, Immanuel Kant prophesied that mankind would one day be faced with a dilemma: either to be joined in a true union of nations or to perish in a war of annihilation ending in the extinction of the human race. Now, as we move from the second to the third millennium, the hour has struck the moment of truth.

In this respect the year 1990 represents a watershed. It marks the end of the unnatural division of Europe. Germany has been reunited. We have begun resolutely to tear down the material foundations of a military, political, and ideological confrontation. But there are some very grave threats that have not been eliminated: the potential for conflict and the primitive instances which allow it, aggressive intentions, and totalitarian traditions. . . .

The Nobel Peace Prize for 1990 confirms that *perestroika* and our new political thinking no longer belong only to us, the people of the Soviet Union. Rather they are the property of the whole of mankind and are an inseparable part of its destiny and of a safe, peaceful future. We are deeply grateful to Norway and to other members of the international community who have shown such understanding and who, through their conduct in international issues and in their relations with the Soviet Union, have shown their solidarity as we proceed with our *perestroika* and their sympathy as we struggle to resolve our problems. If we all took this as our point of departure, mankind would have no cause to regret the loss of a unique opportunity for reason and the logic of peace to prevail over that of war and alienation.

Gorbachev has told the committee that he will present his Nobel lecture in May 1991. Perhaps by then internal developments in the Soviet Union may indicate whether it is the pessimists or the optimists who are right. But whatever may come to pass, Gorbachev's achievements on the world scene would seem to have secured him his place in history. He will be remembered, as a member of the Nobel Committee put it, as "the man who thawed the ice." ■

*Nobel laureates Harry Markowitz, William Sharpe and Merton Miller talked during a reception in Stockholm.*

# THE ALFRED NOBEL MEMORIAL PRIZE IN ECONOMIC SCIENCES

## THE WORK OF PROFESSOR HARRY M. MARKOWITZ, PROFESSOR MERTON H. MILLER, AND PROFESSOR WILLIAM F. SHARPE

*Before the 1950s, there was hardly any theory whatsoever of financial markets. A pioneering contribution in the field was made by Harry Markowitz. Merton Miller, with Franco Modigliani, founded the modern theory of corporate finance, and William Sharpe developed the Capital Asset Pricing Model for investors.*
*—Professor Assar Lindbeck, member of the Royal Swedish Academy of Sciences and the Prize Committee for the Alfred Nobel Memorial Prize in Economic Sciences.*

In past years economists have often found it difficult to explain to nonprofessionals what the winners of the Nobel Prize had done to deserve the honor or how they had changed lives in Paris or Peoria—but not this year. Harry M. Markowitz, Merton H. Miller, and William F. Sharpe, the three academic researchers who shared the 1990 prize, are the intellectual progenitors of a field of economics called finance, a field that offers insights about, and sometimes even answers to, very practical questions: How much more should you pay for a rock-solid stock than for shares in a company with volatile earnings? Can anyone consistently beat the stock market without taking large risks? How much corporate debt is too much?

At the age of sixty-three, Harry Markowitz is still a busy teacher of finance (at the City University of New

York's Baruch College), a computer whiz (he developed a computer language that is still used), and a consultant (to Daiwa Securities). But his Nobel-winning work came early in his career, even before he earned his doctorate at the University of Chicago in 1955.

Before Markowitz, stock market analysts certainly knew that asset diversification was generally a virtue—that prudent money managers hardly ever put all their eggs in one basket. But it took the mild-mannered Chicago-born researcher to substitute mathematical rigor for intuition, and in the process, he transformed stock picking from an art to a science.

*Markowitz developed a theory of portfolio decisions.*

According to Markowitz the income from assets—for simplicity, only stocks will be considered here—had two critical dimensions: the likely (or expected) return and the range of possible returns, technically measured as statistical variance. Everyone wants the highest possible expected return: 20 percent annually on stocks is unambiguously better than 10 percent. But at the same time, everyone—except high-rolling gamblers—wishes to keep variance to a minimum. Both Du Pont and the Ouagadougou Fertilizer and Storm Door Corporation may have equally good prospects of doubling their earnings over the next five years. But people who like to sleep at night will pay more for ownership of a dollar's worth of Du Pont's annual earnings because there is less risk of a loss.

Markowitz's great insight was that proper packaging of assets could reduce the variance of earnings of an investor's portfolio without reducing the expected return. For example, an investor in General Motors (GM) would not get much benefit from diversifying into Ford stock because many of the sources of uncertainty affecting Ford's future earnings—gasoline prices, interest rates, economic growth—are closely related to the uncertainties affecting GM's earnings. But the owner of GM shares could have his cake and eat it too by diversifying into Royal Dutch Petroleum. An off year for GM would not necessarily mean hard times for Royal Dutch. Indeed, the high oil prices that hammered GM's earnings would almost certainly mean exceptional profits for the energy giant.

A 1952 journal article by Markowitz laid

*On a sightseeing tour of Stockholm, Markowitz paused to inspect a display of Swedish crystal.*

out the mathematics for assembling port-folios with the optimal diversification characteristics, portfolios that gave inves-tors the highest expected return for a given level of variance. And MBAs wielding spreadsheets have been busy ever since, calculating "optimal" portfolios from stocks, bonds, options, and futures. Even small investors can now get in on the action by using special programs developed for per-sonal computers to play the markets or by purchasing shares in mutual funds that specialize in Markowitz-inspired number-crunching.

This was quite an accomplishment in itself. In fact, Markowitz's idea for valuing assets on the basis of expected return and variance of return became the rock on which an entire subfield of economics was built. One builder was James Tobin, the Yale University scholar whose 1958 work in expanding the concepts of portfolio theory helped earn him a Nobel Memorial Prize in 1982. Another was William Sharpe, a graduate student at the University of California at Los Angeles (UCLA) in the late 1950s who labored at the side of Harry Markowitz, then a researcher at the Rand Corporation up the road in Santa Monica.

Sharpe convinced the UCLA economics department to let Markowitz direct Sharpe's doctoral thesis. The completed research, published in 1963 and 1964, when he was teaching finance at the University of Washington in Seattle, made Sharpe a star scholar at the ripe old age of thirty. From Seattle he went to Stanford, with a brief stop at the University of California at Irvine. Sharpe is still associated with Stanford's Graduate School of Business. But he spends much of his energies as the head of a consulting firm, William F. Sharpe Associates, that applies computerized evaluation techniques to the investment problems of pension funds.

*Miller co-founded the modern theory of corporate finance.*

The Royal Swedish Academy of Sciences cites Sharpe for the formulation of a generalization of portfolio theory called the Capital Asset Pricing Model (CAPM). In fact, CAPM, as it is known today, is an explosion of good ideas from a half-dozen scholars, each connected to the others. Sharpe's paper, written in 1962, was an outgrowth of his thesis.

Recall that Markowitz's portfolio theory gave investors a way to compute the best available trade-offs between securities with higher risk (variance) and higher expected return. The CAPM developers pointed out the unintuitive truth that as long as security markets were easily accessible to all, investors would all choose the same point on the curve—the identical combination of risk and expected return—even though the willingness to take chances might vary greatly from investor to investor.

The mix of assets that creates this particular combination of risk and likely reward is called the "optimal portfolio." An investor who considers the optimal portfolio too risky will find that the best way to reduce risk at minimal loss of return is not to move along the Markowitz risk-return curve but to combine a piece of optimal portfolio with a riskless asset. If, for example, a conservative investor had $100,000, he might put $20,000 in the optimal portfolio of stocks and bonds and lend the other $80,000 risklessly to the U.S. Treasury by purchasing T-bills.

Suppose, instead, that an investor preferred to bear more risk in pursuit of profit than the optimal portfolio afforded. He would discover that the way to get the

*After the Nobel Prize ceremony, Miller rejoined his wife, Katherine, and their daughter.*

biggest bang on expected return for a risky investment would be to buy extra amounts of the optimal portfolio with borrowed funds—leveraging, say, $300,000 worth of the portfolio with $100,000 in cash and a $200,000 loan.

Now, if all well-informed investors buy the same mix of risky assets—no matter how conservative (or risk-tolerant) their investment objectives might be—it follows that all assets must be in the optimal portfolio; otherwise, no sensible person would own the assets in question. How can that be? Easy, said Sharpe. The price of each asset must adjust in the marketplace until the expected return is just high enough

to offset the additional risk created when it is added to the optimal portfolio.

Remember that it is not always obvious how much risk any given asset will add to the brew. An asset with very volatile earnings might add no risk at all if the pattern of volatility is offset by the pattern of volatility of the rest of the portfolio. Only the computers know for sure.

Perhaps the most useful—and surely the most famous—idea to come out of CAPM is Sharpe's distinction between systematic and unsystematic risk. Systematic risk is risk that cannot be diversified away. Its measure, or "beta," is proportional to the volatility of the market as a whole. If, for example, a stock has a beta of 1.3, it is likely to go up 13 percent when, on average, stocks go up 10 percent. By the same token, a stock with a beta of 1.3 is likely to fall by 13 percent when the stock market falls by 10 percent.

An asset is overpriced, Sharpe said, if the excess expected return over that of T-bills compared to that from the market as a whole is not roughly proportional to its beta. Thus, a mutual fund with a beta of 1.5 (a risky portfolio, indeed) is not a bargain unless the excess return averages at least 1.5 times that of the market, but a fund with a beta of .7 might well underperform

*Sharpe explained how asset prices are determined.*

the market in a good year and still be viewed as well managed.

Beta is not without its critics. For one thing, the basic analysis is no better than the simplifying assumptions that underlie it, and some economists think the assumptions distort reality in important ways. For another, beta is hard to measure. The numbers generated by the computers show what beta was in the past, not what it is today; if the statistical characteristics of the asset are in flux, the number will not mean much.

But even the critics concede that the measurement of systematic risk is central to the issue of valuing risky assets. All that is really left to debate is how best to manage and interpret the measurement.

At first glance, Merton Miller's great contribution to economics, the Modigliani-Miller theorem, seems unrelated to portfolio theory and CAPM. Miller and his co-theorist, Franco Modigliani, who won a Nobel Memorial Prize in 1985, wrote about the investment decisions of corporations, not the portfolio decisions of investors. But as we shall see, "M-M," as it is known in finance, is a kissing cousin to CAPM.

The story begins in 1958, when the thirty-five-year-old Miller, a Johns Hopkins Ph.D. tax expert, was teaching at Carnegie-Mellon University in Pittsburgh. Like Modigliani, who occupied the adjoining office, he was interested in the relationship between corporations' capital structures and their share values.

At the time, it was widely assumed that there was some optimal degree of corporate leverage, some optimal balance be-

*At a reception and press conference at the Academy of Sciences, Sharpe fielded questions from the podium.*

tween debt and share equity. With too little debt, corporations would be passing up opportunities to raise funds at low rates, which would enhance the value of the stock. Yet, with too much debt, corporations would have lenders raising interest charges and anxious investors fleeing the stock for more conservative corporate climes. The trick, it seemed, was to balance the costs of borrowing money against the costs of diluting share values by selling additional stock.

But Modigliani and Miller, who later moved on to the University of Chicago Business School, believed that if investors can create something on their own, they

won't pay more to have a corporation provide it for them. Likewise, if investors felt the stock was underleveraged, they could leverage it up by borrowing on their own. Thus, the debt-to-equity ratio of a corporation and the resulting change in the volatility of its earnings should not be relevant to the value of shares.

An example will clarify this. Consider the Fly-by-Nite Airline, which runs its business with $100 million worth of equipment and a whopping $95 million in debt. Fly-by-Nite is obviously a high roller: Even modest changes in revenue are likely to spell the difference between a big loss and a profit bonanza. One might thus expect conservative investors to avoid the stock, putting a lid on its share value.

But, as M-M suggests, that need not be the case in a world of well-developed capital markets. A conservative investor who thinks that Fly-by-Nite's prospects (its expected return) are good can improve his overall return without bearing unacceptable risks, by mixing Fly-by-Nite shares with a riskless asset, such as insured CDs or T-bills. Thus, just as Sharpe showed that unsystematic risk is irrelevant to asset values, M-M showed that a company's debt-to-equity ratio should be irrelevant to its stock price.

By the same logic, M-M said, a company's policy on dividend payments should be unrelated to the share value. An investor who wishes a company would pay out a higher percentage of income in cash can always mix the stock with higher-yield securities or use the stock as collateral to borrow. An investor who has little need for dividends can always include some low-dividend shares in his stock portfolio or lend out the dividend income to those who need cash more.

If you smell a rat here, you are not alone. The publication of the original M-M theorem in 1958 (with extensions in 1963) was greeted with incredulity by almost everyone in the investment industry. Debt-to-equity ratios must matter, they insisted, and so, too, must dividend policies.

They were right. As a hundred subsequent research papers showed, the validity of M-M depends on a series of assumptions that do not hold up in the real world. Debt-to-equity ratios do matter because highly indebted companies are more likely to go bankrupt, and in the process of reorganizing the corporation or liquidating its assets, there is a real loss of productivity. Dividend policies do matter because corporate earnings escape double taxation as long as they are retained by the corporation.

But this does not undermine the intel-

---

### HOW WILL THESE ECONOMISTS INVEST THEIR PRIZE MONEY?
#### (Interviews)

Asked what he planned to do with the shared Prize, about $207,000 each, Markowitz said, "We are going to do something a little mad, and then take the rest and put it in the portfolio. I'm going to sound-proof a room so I can play my music up at concert level and not disturb my wife. That would be my mad money.

"Money is money, and you put it into the fund, and you diversify—maybe a third of it into equities and a third of it into bonds and another third of it into real estate raw land. . . ."

Miller said, "I would plan to invest it. We believe in diversification—just hold a wide variety of things."

Sharpe said, "I'm going to devote what's left—after taxes, of course—primarily to research, to buy some more data bases and that sort of thing."

lectual triumph of M-M. Like many important theories in economics, the framework for reasoning matters more than predictive power. M-M fundamentally changed the way economists think about corporate financial structure, focusing attention on the factors that really do affect share values. Without Markowitz, Sharpe, Miller, and a handful of other economists who incorporated concepts of risk into asset valuation, there would be no modern field of finance. ■

*The diplomas for the laureates include original art work.*

*The center table at the December 10 banquet was reserved for honored guests.*

# LIST OF NOBEL LAUREATES 1901-1990

| Year | Physics | Chemistry | Physiology or Medicine | Literature | Peace |
|------|---------|-----------|------------------------|------------|-------|
| 1901 | W. C. Rontgen (G) | J. H. van't Hoff (Nl) | E. A. von Behring (G) | Sully Prudhomme (F) | J. H. Dunant (Swi)<br>F. Passy (F) |
| 1902 | H. A. Lorentz (Nl)<br>P. Zeeman (Nl) | H. E. Fischer (G) | R. Ross (GB) | Theodor Mommsen (G) | E. Ducommun (Swi)<br>C. A. Gobat (Swi) |
| 1903 | A. H. Becquerel (F)<br>P. Curie (F)<br>M. Curie (F) | S. A. Arrhenius (Swe) | N. R. Finsen (D) | Björnstjerne Björnson (N) | W. R. Cremer (GB) |
| 1904 | J. W. S. Rayleigh (GB) | W. Ramsey (GB) | I. P. Pavlov (R) | Frederic Mistral (F)<br>Jose Echegaray (Sp) | Institute of International Law, Ghent |
| 1905 | P. E. A. Lenard (G) | J. F. W. A. von Baeyer (G) | R. Koch (G) | Henryk Sienkiewicz (Pol) | B. S. F. von Suttner (Au) |
| 1906 | J. J. Thomson (GB) | H. Moissan (F) | C. Golgi (I)<br>S. Ramon y Cajal (Sp) | Giouse Carducci (I) | T. Roosevelt (US) |
| 1907 | A. A. Michelson (US) | E. Buchner (G) | C. L. A. Laveran (F) | Rudyard Kipling (GB) | E. T. Moneta (I)<br>L. Renault (F) |
| 1908 | G. Lippman (F) | E. Rutherford (GB) | P. Ehrlich (G)<br>I. Mecnikov (R) | Rudolf Eucken (G) | K. P. Arnoldson (Swe)<br>F. Bajer (D) |
| 1909 | G. Marconi (I)<br>C. F. Braun (G) | W. Ostwald (G) | E. T. Kocher (Swi) | Selma Lagerlof (Swe) | A. M. F. Beernaert (B)<br>P. H. B. B. d'Estournelles de Constant (F) |
| 1910 | J. D. van der Waals (Nl) | O. Wallach (G) | A. Kossel (G) | Paul Heyse (G) | Permanent International Peace Bureau, Berne |
| 1911 | W. Wien (G) | M. Curie (F) | A. Gullstrand (Swe) | Maurice Maeterlinck (B) | T. M. C. Asser (Nl)<br>A. H. Fried (Au) |
| 1912 | N. G. Dalen (Swe) | V. Grignard (F)<br>P. Sabatier (F) | A. Carrel (F) | Gerhart Hauptmann (G) | E. Root (US) |
| 1913 | H. Kamerlingh-Onnes (Nl) | A. Werner (Swi) | C. R. Richet (F) | Rabindranath Tagore (In) | H. La Fontaine (B) |
| 1914 | M. von Laue (G) | T. W. Richards (US) | R. Barany (H) | Not awarded | Not awarded |
| 1915 | W. H. Bragg (GB)<br>W. L. Bragg (GB) | R. M. Willstater (G) | Not awarded | Romain Rolland (F) | Not awarded |
| 1916 | Not awarded | Not awarded | Not awarded | Verner v. Heidenstram (Swe) | Not awarded |
| 1917 | C. G. Barkla (GB) | Not awarded | Not awarded | Karl Gjellerup (D)<br>Henrik Pontoppidan (D) | International Committee of the Red Cross, Geneva |
| 1918 | M. K. E. L. Planck (G) | F. Haber (G) | Not awarded | Not awarded | Not awarded |
| 1919 | J. Stark (G) | Not awarded | J. Bordet (B) | Carl Spitteler (Swi) | T. W. Wilson (US) |
| 1920 | C. E. Guillaume (Swi) | W. H. Nernst (G) | S. A. S. Krogh (D) | Knut Hamsun (N) | L. V. A. Bourgeois (F) |
| 1921 | A. Einstein (G/Swi) | F. Soddy (GB) | Not awarded | Anatole France (F) | K. H. Branting (Swe)<br>C. L. Lange (N) |
| 1922 | N. Bohr (D) | F. W. Aston (GB) | A. V. Hill (GB)<br>O. F. Meyerhof (G) | Jaconto Benavente (Sp) | F. Nansen (N) |
| 1923 | R. A. Millikan (US) | F. Pregl (Au) | F. G. Banting (Ca)<br>J. J. R. Macleod (Ca) | W. B. Yeats (Ir) | Not awarded |
| 1924 | K. M. G. Siegbahn (Swe) | Not awarded | W. Einthoven (Nl) | Wladyslaw Reymont (Pol) | Not awarded |
| 1925 | J. Franck (G)<br>G. Hertz (G) | R. A. Zsigmondy (G) | Not awarded | G. B. Shaw (GB) | J. A. Chamberlain (GB)<br>C. G. Dawes (US) |
| 1926 | J. B. Perrin (F) | T. Svedberg (Swe) | J. A. G. Fibiger (D) | Grazia Deledda (I) | A. Briand (F)<br>G. Stresemann (G) |
| 1927 | A. H. Compton (US)<br>C. T. R. Wilson (GB) | H. O. Wieland (G) | J. Wagner-Jauregg (Au) | Henri Bergson (F) | F. Buisson (F)<br>L. Quidde (G) |
| 1928 | O.W. Richardson (GB) | A. O. R. Windaus (G) | C. J. H. Nicolle (F) | Sigrid Undset (N) | Not awarded |
| 1929 | L. V. de Broglie (F) | A. Harden (GB)<br>H. K. A. S. von Euler-Chelpin (Swe) | C. Eijkman (Nl)<br>F. G. Hopkins (GB) | Thomas Mann (G) | F. B. Kellog (US) |
| 1930 | C. V. Raman (In) | H. Fischer (G) | K. Landsteiner (Au) | Sinclair Lewis (US) | L. O. N. Soderblom (Swe) |
| 1931 | Not awarded | C. Bosch (G)<br>F. Bergius (G) | O. H. Warburg (G) | Erik Axel Karlfeldt (Swe) | J. Addams (US)<br>N. M. Butler (US) |
| 1932 | W. Heisenberg (G) | I. Langmuir (US) | C. S. Sherrington (GB)<br>E. D. Adrian (GB) | John Galsworthy (GB) | Not awarded |
| 1933 | E. Schrodinger (Au)<br>P. A. M. Dirac (GB) | Not awarded | T. H. Morgan (US) | Ivan Bunin (stateless) | N. R. L. Angell (GB) |
| 1934 | Not awarded | H. C. Urey (US) | G. H. Whipple (US)<br>W. P. Murphy (US)<br>G. R. Minot (US) | Luigi Pirandello (I) | A. Henderson (GB) |
| 1935 | J. Chadwick (GB) | F. Joliot (F)<br>I. Joliot-Curie (F) | H. Spemann (G) | Not awarded | C. von Ossietzky (G) |
| 1936 | V. F. Hess (Au)<br>C. D. Anderson (US) | P. J. W. Debye (Nl) | H. H. Dale (GB)<br>O. Loewi (Au) | Eugene O'Neill (US) | C. Saavedra Lamas (Ar) |
| 1937 | C. J. Davisson (US)<br>G. P. Thomson (GB) | W. N. Haworth (GB)<br>P. Karrer (Swi) | A. Szent-Gyorgyi von Nagyrapolt (H) | Roger Martin du Gard (F) | E. A. R. G. Cecil (GB) |

| Year | Physics | Chemistry | Physiology or Medicine | Literature | Peace |
|------|---------|-----------|------------------------|------------|-------|
| 1938 | E. Fermi (I) | R. Kuhn (G) | C. J. F. Heymans (B) | Pearl Buck (US) | Nansen International Office for Refugees, Geneva |
| 1939 | E. O. Lawrence (US) | A. F. J. Butenandt (G) L. Ruzicka (Swi) | G. Domagk (G) | F. E. Sillanpaa (Fi) | Not awarded |
| 1940 | Not awarded | Not awarded | Not awarded | Not awarded | Not awarded |
| 1941 | Not awarded | Not awarded | Not awarded | Not awarded | Not awarded |
| 1942 | Not awarded | Not awarded | Not awarded | Not awarded | Not awarded |
| 1943 | O. Stern (US) | G. de Hevsey (H) | E. A. Doisy (US) H. C. P. Dam (D) | Not awarded | Not awarded |
| 1944 | I. I. Rabi (US) | O. Hahn (G) | J. Erlanger (US) H. S. Gasser (US) | Johannes V. Jensen (D) | International Committee of the Red Cross, Geneva |
| 1945 | W. Pauli (Au) | A. I. Virtanen (Fi) | A. Fleming (GB) E. B. Chain (GB) H. W. Florey (GB) | Gabriela Mistral (Chile) | C. Hull (US) |
| 1946 | P.W. Bridgman (US) | J. B. Sumner (US) J. H. Northrop (US) W. M. Stanley (US) | H. J. Muller (US) | Hermann Hesse (Swi) | E. G. Balch (US) J. R. Mott (US) |
| 1947 | E.V. Appleton (GB) | R. Robinson (GB) | C. F. Cori (US) G. T. Cori (US) B. A. Houssay (Ar) | André Gide (F) | The Friends Service Council (GB) The American Friends Service Committee (US) |
| 1948 | P.M. S. Blackett (GB) | A. W. K. Tiselius (Swe) | P. H. Muller (Swi) | T. S. Eliot (GB) | |
| 1949 | H. Yukawa (J) | W. F. Giauque (US) | A. C. de Abreu Freire Egas Moniz (Por) W. R. Hess (Swi) | William Faulkner (US) | Not awarded J. Boyd Orr (GB) |
| 1950 | C.F. Powell (GB) | O. P. H. Diels (FRG) K. Alder (FRG) | P. S. Hench (US) E. C. Kendall (US) T. Reichstein (Swi) | Bertrand Russell (GB) | R. Bunche (US) |
| 1951 | J.D. Cockcroft (GB) E. T. S. Walton (Ir) | E. M. McMillan (US) G. T. Seaborg (US) | M. Theiler (SA) | Pär Lagerkvist (Swe) | L. Jouhaux (F) |
| 1952 | F. Bloch (US) E. M. Purcell (US) | A. J. P. Martin (GB) R. L. M. Synge (GB) | S. A. Waksman (US) | Francois Mauriac (F) | A. Schweitzer (F/G) |
| 1953 | F. Zernike (Nl) | H. Staudinger (FRG) | H. A. Krebs (GB) F. A. Lipmann (US) | Winston Churchill (GB) | G. C. Marshall (US) |
| 1954 | M. Born (GB) W. Bothe (FRG) | L. C. Pauling (US) | J. F. Enders (US) T. H. Weller (US) F. C. Robbins (US) | Ernest Hemingway (US) | Office of the United Nations' High Commissioner for Refugees, Geneva |
| 1955 | W. E. Lamb (US) P. Kusch (US) | V. du Vigneaud (US) | A. H. T. Theorell (Swe) | Halldor Laxness (Ic) | Not awarded |
| 1956 | W. Schockley (US) J. Bardeen (US) W. H. Brattain (US) | C. N. Hinshelwood (GB) N. N. Semenov (USSR) | A. F. Cournand (US) W. Forssmann (FRG) D. W. Richard Jr. (US) | J. R. Jimenez (Sp) | Not awarded |
| 1957 | C. N. Yang (China) T. D. Lee (China) | A. R. Todd (GB) | D. Bovet (I) | Albert Camus (F) | L. B. Pearson (Ca) |
| 1958 | P. A. Cerenkov (USSR) I. M. Frank (USSR) I. J. Tamm (USSR) | F. Sanger (GB) | G. W. Beadle (US) E. L. Tatum (US) J. Lederberg (US) | Boris Pasternak (USSR) (declined the prize) | G. Pire (B) |
| 1959 | E. G. Segre (US) O. Chamberlain (US) | J. Heyrovsky (Cz) | S. Ochoa (US) A. Kornberg (US) | Salvatore Quasimodo (I) | P. J. Noel-Baker (GB) |
| 1960 | D. A. Glaser (US) | W. F. Libby (US) | F. M. Burnet (Austr) P. B. Medawar (GB) | Saint-John Perse (F) | A. J. Luthuli (SA) |
| 1961 | R. Hofstadter (US) R. L. Mossbauer (FRG) | M. Calvin (US) | G. von Bekesy (US) | Ivo Andric (Y) | D. H. A. C. Hammarskjold (Swe) |
| 1962 | L. D. Landau (USSR) | M. F. Perutz (GB) J. C. Kendrew (GB) | F. H. C. Crick (GB) J. D. Watson (US) M. H. F. Wilkins (GB) | John Steinbeck (US) | L. C. Pauling (US) |
| 1963 | E. P. Wigner (US) M. Goeppert-Mayer (US) J. H. D. Jensen (FRG) | K. Ziegler (FRG) G. Natta (I) | J. C. Eccles (Austr) A. L. Hodgkin (GB) A. F. Huxley (GB) | Giorgos Seferis (Gr) | International Committee of the Red Cross, Geneva League of Red Cross Societies, Geneva |
| 1964 | Ch. H. Townes (US) N. G. Basov (USSR) A. M. Prochorov (USSR) | D. Crowfoot Hodgkin (GB) | K. Bloch (US) F. Lynen (FRG) | Jean-Paul Sartre (F) (declined the prize) | M. L. King (US) |
| 1965 | S. I. Tomonaga (J) J. Schwinger (US) R. P. Feynman (US) | R. B. Woodward (US) | F. Jacob (F) A. Lwoff (F) J. Monod (F) | Mikhail Sholokov (USSR) | United Nation's Children's Fund (UNICEF) |
| 1966 | A. Kastler (F) | R. S. Mulliken (US) | P. Rous (US) C. B. Huggins (US) | Shmuel Y. Agnon (Is) Nelly Sachs (G) | Not awarded |

| Year | Physics | Chemistry | Physiology or Medicine | Literature | Peace |
|------|---------|-----------|------------------------|------------|-------|
| 1967 | H. A. Bethe (US) | M. Eigen (FRG)<br>R. G. W. Norrish (GB)<br>G. Porter (GB) | R. Granit (Swe)<br>H. K. Hartline (US)<br>G. Wald (US) | Miguel A. Asturias (Guat) | Not awarded |
| 1968 | L. W. Alvarez (US) | L. Onsager (US) | R. W. Holley (US)<br>H. G. Khorana (US)<br>M. W. Nirenberg (US) | Yasunari Kawabata (J) | R. Cassin (F) |
| 1969 | M. Gell-Mann (US) | D. H. R. Barton (GB)<br>O. Hassel (N) | M. Delbrück (US)<br>A. D. Hershey (US)<br>S. E. Luria (US) | Samuel Beckett (Ir) | International Labor<br>Organization, Geneva |
| 1970 | H. Alfven (Swe)<br>L. Neel (F) | L. Leloir (Ar) | B. Katz (GB)<br>U. von Euler (Swe)<br>J. Axelrod (US) | Alexander Solzhenitsyn (USSR) | N. E. Borlaug (US) |
| 1971 | D. Gabor (GB) | G. Herzberg (Ca) | E. W. Sutherland (US) | Pablo Neruda (Chile) | W. Brandt (FRG) |
| 1972 | J. Bardeen (US)<br>L. N. Cooper (US)<br>J. R. Schrieffer (US) | Ch. B. Anfinsen (US)<br>S. Moore (US)<br>W. H. Stein (US) | G. M. Edelman (US)<br>R. R. Porter (GB) | Heinrich Boll (FRG) | Not awarded |
| 1973 | L. Esaki (J)<br>I. Giaever (US)<br>B. D. Josephson (GB) | E. O. Fischer (FRG)<br>G. Wilkinson (GB) | K. von Frisch (FRG)<br>K. Lorenz (Au)<br>N. Tinbergen (GB) | Patrick White (Austr) | H. A. Kissinger (US)<br>Le Duc Tho (Vietnam)<br>(declined the prize) |
| 1974 | M. Ryle (GB)<br>A. Hewish (GB) | P. J. Flory (US) | A. Claude (B)<br>C. de Duve (B)<br>G. E. Palade (US | Eyvind Johnson (Swe)<br>Harry Martinson (Swe) | S. MacBride (Ir)<br>E. Sato (J) |
| 1975 | A. Bohr (D)<br>B. Mottelson (D)<br>J. Rainwater (US) | J. W. Cornforth (GB)<br>V. Prelog (Swi) | D. Baltimore (US)<br>R. Dulbecco (US)<br>H. M. Temin (US) | Eugenio Montale (I) | A. Sakharov (USSR) |
| 1976 | B. Richter (US)<br>S. C. C. Ting (US) | W. N. Lipscomb (US) | B. S. Blumberg (US)<br>D. C. Gajdusek (US) | Saul Bellow (US) | M. Corrigan (GB)<br>B. Williams (GB) |
| 1977 | P. W. Anderson (US)<br>N. F. Mott (GB)<br>J. H. Van Vleck (US) | I. Prigogine (B) | R. Guillemin (US)<br>A. Schally (US)<br>R. Yalow (US) | Vincente Aleixandre (Sp) | Amnesty International |
| 1978 | P. L. Kapitsa (USSR)<br>A. A. Penzias (US)<br>R. W. Wilson (US) | P. Mitchell (GB) | W. Arber (Swi)<br>D. Nathans (US)<br>H. O. Smith (US) | Isaac B. Singer (US) | M. Begin (Is)<br>A. Sadat (Egypt) |
| 1979 | S. L. Glashow (US)<br>A. Salam (Pak)<br>S. Weinberg (US) | H. C. Brown (US)<br>G. Wittig (FRG) | A. M. Cormack (US)<br>G. N. Hounsfield (GB) | Odysseus Elytis (Gr) | Mother Teresa (In) |
| 1980 | J. W. Cronin (US)<br>V. L. Fitch (US) | P. Berg (US)<br>W. Gilbert (US)<br>F. Sanger (GB) | B. Benacerraf (US)<br>J. Dausset (F)<br>G. D. Snell (US) | Czeslaw Milosz (Pol/US) | A. Perez Esquivel (Ar) |
| 1981 | N. Bloembergen (US)<br>A. L. Schawlow (US)<br>K. M. Siegbahn (Swe) | K. Fukui (J)<br>R. Hoffman (US) | D. H. Hubel (US)<br>R. W. Sperry (US)<br>T. N. Wiesel (Swe) | Elias Canetti (GB) | Office of the United Nations'<br>High Commissioner for<br>Refugees, Geneva |
| 1982 | K. G. Wilson (US) | A. Klug (GB) | S. Bergström (Swe)<br>B. I. Samuelsson (Swe)<br>J. R. Vane (GB) | Gabriel García Márquez ( Co) | A. Myrdal (Swe)<br>A. Garcia Robles (M) |
| 1983 | S. Chandrasekhar (US)<br>W. A. Fowler (US) | H. Taube (US) | B. McClintock (US) | William Golding (GB) | L. Walesa (Pol) |
| 1984 | C. Rubbia (I)<br>S. van der Meer (Nl) | B. Merrifield (US) | N. K. Jerne (D)<br>G. J. F. Köhler (FRG)<br>C. Milstein (GB/Ar) | Jaroslav Seifert (Cz) | D. Tutu (SA) |
| 1985 | K. von Klitzing (FRG) | H. A. Hauptman (US)<br>J. Karle (US) | M. S. Brown (US)<br>J. L. Goldstein (US) | Claude Simon (F) | Intern. Physicians for the<br>Prevention of Nuclear War |
| 1986 | E. Ruska (FRG)<br>G. Binnig (FRG)<br>H. Rohrer (Swi) | D. R. Herschbach (US)<br>Y. T. Lee (US)<br>J. C. Polanyi (Ca) | S. Cohen (US)<br>R. Levi-Montalcini (I/US) | Wole Soyinka (Ni) | E. Wiesel (US) |
| 1987 | J. G. Bednorz (FRG)<br>K. A. Muller (Swi) | D. J. Cram (US)<br>J. M. Lehn (F)<br>C. J. Pedersen (US) | S. Tonegawa (J) | Joseph Brodsky (US) | O. Arias Sánchez (CR) |
| 1988 | L. M. Lederman (US)<br>M. Schwartz (US)<br>J. Steinberger (US) | J. Diesenhofer (FRG)<br>R. Huber (FRG)<br>H. Michel (FRG) | J. W. Black (GB)<br>G. B. Elion (US)<br>G. H. Hitchings (US) | Naguib Mahfouz (E) | The United Nations Peace-<br>Keeping Forces |
| 1989 | N. F. Ramsey (US)<br>H. G. Dehmelt (US)<br>W. Paul (FRG) | S. Altman (US/Ca)<br>T. R. Cech (US) | J. M. Bishop (US)<br>H. E. Varmus (US) | Camilo José Cela (Sp) | The 14th Dalai Lama (Tenzin<br>Gyatso) (Tib) |
| 1990 | J. I. Friedman (US)<br>H. W. Kendall (US)<br>R. E. Taylor (Ca) | E. J. Corey (US) | J. E. Murray (US)<br>E. D. Thomas (US) | Octavio Paz (M) | M. Gorbachev (USSR) |

# THE BANK OF SWEDEN PRIZE IN ECONOMICS IN MEMORY OF ALFRED NOBEL, LIST OF LAUREATES

| | | | | | | | |
|---|---|---|---|---|---|---|---|
| 1969 | R. Frisch (N) | 1974 | G. Myrdal (Swe) | 1979 | A. Lewis (GB) | 1985 | F. Modigliani (US) |
| | J. Tinbergen (NI) | | F. A. von Hayek (GB) | | T. W. Schultz (US) | 1986 | J. M. Buchanan Jr. (US) |
| 1970 | P. Samuelson (US) | 1975 | L. V. Kantorovich (USSR) | 1980 | L. Klein (US) | 1987 | R. M. Solow (US) |
| 1971 | S. Kuznets (US) | | T. C. Koopmans (US) | 1981 | J. Tobin (US) | 1988 | M. Allais (F) |
| 1972 | J. R. Hicks (GB) | 1976 | M. Friedman (US) | 1982 | G. J. Stigler (US) | 1989 | T. Haavelmo (N) |
| | K. Arrow (US) | 1977 | B. Ohlin (Swe) | 1983 | G. Debreu (US) | 1990 | H. M. Markowitz (US) |
| 1973 | W. Leontief (US) | | J. Meade (GB) | 1984 | R. Stone (GB) | | M. H. Miller (US) |
| | | 1978 | H. Simon (US) | | | | W. F. Sharpe (US) |

## Abbreviations

Ar Argentina; Austr Australia; Au Austria; B Belgium; Ca Canada; Co Colombia; CR Costa Rica; Cz Czechoslovakia; D Denmark; E Egypt; Fi Finland; F France; FRG Federal Republic of Germany; G Germany (before 1948); GB Great Britain; Gr Greece; Guat Guatemala; H Hungary; Ic Iceland; In India; Ir Ireland; Is Israel; I Italy; J Japan; M Mexico; NI The Netherlands; Ni Nigeria; N Norway; Pak Pakistan; Pol Poland; Por Portugal; R Russia (after 1922 USSR); Sp Spain; Swe Sweden; Swi Switzerland; SA Republic of South Africa; Tib Tibet; US United States; Y Yugoslavia.

# IN MEMORIAM

PAVEL ALEKSEJVIC CERENOV, USSR (1904-1990)

1958 Laureate in Physics

_____

IL'JA MICHAJLOVIC FRANK, USSR (1908-1990)

1958 Laureate in Physics

_____

PATRICK WHITE, Australia (1912-1990)

1973 Laureate in Literature

# About the Authors

### BARON STIG RAMEL

Stig Ramel has since 1972 been Executive Director of the Nobel Foundation. He was vice president, later president, of the General Swedish Export Association from 1966-1972 and is chairman, vice chairman or board member of eighteen Swedish and international companies and organizations. From 1953 to 1966, he worked for the Swedish Ministry for Foreign Affairs and served as a diplomat at the embassies in Paris and Washington.

### WILLIAM A. HENRY III

William A. Henry III, a senior writer at *Time*, has been the magazine's theater critic since January 1985. In 1980, he won a Pulitzer Prize in "distinguished criticism." He has contributed to other magazines including *Life, Esquire, Smithsonian, The New Republic* and *Washington Journalism Review*. He wrote an Emmy-winning hour documentary special for PBS, "Bob Fosse: Steam Heat," which aired in February 1990. Henry, a graduate of Yale, has taught at Yale and Tufts universities and lectured at Harvard, Columbia, MIT, and more than a dozen other colleges.

### SHARON BEGLEY

Sharon Begley has been the science editor of *Newsweek* magazine since 1982, where she reports and writes on subjects ranging from astronomy to zoology, space science to science policy. She has also taught environmental reporting at the Columbia University Graduate School of Journalism.

### RICHARD WOLKOMIR

Richard Wolkomir is a recipient of the American Association for the Advancement of Science/Westinghouse Award for Distinguished Science Writing. He contributes to many U.S. magazines including *Smithsonian, Air & Space* and *Reader's Digest*.

### MARTHA FAY

Martha Fay, a former reporter and writer for *Life* and *Time* magazines, often specializes in medical subjects. She is the author of *A Mortal Condition*, a book about the lives and treatment of eight cancer patients.

## HERBERT MITGANG

Herbert Mitgang, a daily book critic for the *New York Times*, has inteviewed Octavio Paz several times in recent years. Mitgang is author of a dozen books in the fields of history, biography, and literature. He is a member of the board of directors of the Society of American Historians and serves as president of the Authors League Fund, a charitable foundation.

## IRWIN ABRAMS

Irwin Abrams, author of *The Nobel Peace Prize and the Laureates* (1988), is the world's foremost historian of the Nobel Peace Prize. He is distinguished university professor emeritus at Antioch University and a prominent scholar and practitioner in the field of international education. A lifelong peace advocate, he participated in the world wartime relief and postwar reconstruction work of the American Friends Service Committee, joint winner of the 1947 Nobel Peace Prize.

## PETER PASSELL

Peter Passell, financial columnist for the *New York Times*, wrote the article about the 1990 laureates in economics that appeared in that newspaper.